DANIEL

BRINGING THE BIBLE TO LIFE

Genesis, by John H. Walton, Janet Nygren, and Karen H. Jobes
  (12 sessions)

Esther, by Karen H. Jobes and Janet Nygren
  (8 sessions)

Psalms, by Gerald Wilson, Janet Nygren, and Karen H. Jobes
  (10 sessions) — summer 2010

Daniel, by Tremper Longman III, Janet Nygren, and Karen H. Jobes
  (10 sessions)

Mark, by David E. Garland, Karen-Lee Thorp, and Karen H. Jobes
  (12 sessions)

John, by Gary M. Burge, Karen Lee-Thorp, and Karen H. Jobes
  (12 sessions)

Acts, by Ajith Fernando, Karen Lee-Thorp, and Karen H. Jobes
  (12 sessions) — summer 2010

Romans, by Douglas J. Moo, Karen Lee-Thorp, and Karen H. Jobes
  (12 sessions)

Galatians, by Scot McKnight, Karen Lee-Thorp, and Karen H. Jobes
  (6 sessions)

Ephesians, by Klyne Snodgrass, Karen Lee-Thorp, and Karen H. Jobes
  (6 sessions)

Hebrews, by George H. Guthrie, Janet Nygren, and Karen H. Jobes
  (8 sessions)

Revelation, by Craig S. Keener, Janet Nygren, and Karen H. Jobes
  (10 sessions) — summer 2010

BRINGING
THE
BIBLE
TO LIFE

DANIEL

Faith Under Pressure

Tremper Longman III
and Janet Nygren

Karen H. Jobes, Series Editor

ZONDERVAN®

ZONDERVAN.com/
AUTHORTRACKER
follow your favorite authors

ZONDERVAN

Daniel
Copyright © 2010 by Tremper Longman III, Janet Nygren, and Karen H. Jobes

Requests for information should be addressed to:
Zondervan, *Grand Rapids, Michigan 49530*

ISBN 978-0-310-32042-5

Cover design: Tammy Johnson
Cover and interior photography: Gettyimages, BiblePlaces, The Bridgeman Art Library
Interior design: Michelle Espinoza

Printed in the United States of America

10 11 12 13 14 15 16 • 25 24 23 22 21 20 19 18 17 16 15 14 13 12 11 10 9 8 7 6 5 4 3 2

CONTENTS

SERIES PREFACE

Have you ever been in a small-group Bible study where the leader read a passage from the Bible and then invited the members of the group to share what the passage meant to them? God wants to speak to each person individually through the Bible, but such an approach to a group study can often be a frustrating and shallow experience for both leader and participants. And while the same passage can speak in various ways into people's lives, the meat of the Word is found in what the biblical writer intended to say about God and our relationship to him. The Bringing the Bible to Life series is for those who are ready to move from a surface reading of the Bible into a deeper understanding of God's Word.

But the Bible, though perhaps familiar, was written in ancient languages and in times quite different from our own, so most readers need a bit more help getting to a deeper understanding of its message. A study that begins and ends with what a passage "means to me" leaves the meaning of the passage unanchored and adrift in the thoughts—and perhaps the misunderstanding—of the reader. But who has time to delve into the history, language, cultures, and theology of the Bible? That's the work of biblical scholars who spend their lives researching, teaching, and writing about the ancient Scriptures. The need is to get the fruit of all that research into the hands of those in small-group Bible studies.

Zondervan's NIV Application Commentary (NIVAC) series was written to bring the best of evangelical biblical scholarship to those who want to know *both* the historical meaning of the biblical text *and* its contemporary significance. This companion series, Bringing the Bible to Life, is intended to bring that material into small-group studies in an easy-to-use format. Pastors, Christian education teachers, and small-group leaders whether in church, campus, or home settings will find these guides to be an enriching resource.

Each guide in the series provides an introduction to the biblical book that concisely summarizes the background information needed to better understand the original historical context. Six to twelve sessions per guide, with each session consisting of ten to twelve discussion questions, allow a focused study that moves beyond superficial Bible reading. Relevant excerpts from the corresponding NIVAC commentary provide easy access into additional material for those interested in going even deeper. A closing section in each session assists the group in responding to God's Word together or individually. Guidance for leading each session is included, making the task of small-group leadership more manageable for busy lives.

If you want to move from the biblical text to contemporary life on solid ground, this series has been written for you.

Karen H. Jobes, PhD
Gerald F. Hawthorne Professor of
New Testament Greek and Exegesis
Wheaton College and Graduate School

OF SPECIAL NOTE

Your experience with and understanding of the book of Daniel can be deepened and enriched by referring to the volume on which it is based: *The NIV Application Commentary: Daniel* by Tremper Longman III, published by Zondervan in 1999.

INTRODUCTION[1]

If you ever went to Sunday school as a child, you probably came across some of the beloved stories of Daniel: Daniel and the lions' den; Shadrach, Meshach, and Abednego in the fiery furnace; and the writing on the wall, to name the most well known. You might even remember a catchy tune that went along with a story! But where do these stories fit in history? Or are they just clever stories? What else is in the book of Daniel? How does the book connect to the rest of Scripture? Is there a message in it for us today?

These are important questions—particularly when you realize how far back in history these stories go, how different our culture is from the height of the Babylonian empire, and how our perspectives have changed since the coming of Christ. The gaps make it challenging to come to appropriate conclusions. But we don't want to dismiss them as children's stories. And we don't want to miss out on what they can teach us today.

In fact, Daniel lived in a big city, surrounded by many multicultural influences which had a major impact on his day-to-day life. He had to make choices about what it meant to live out his faith when the rules around him had changed. He faced pressure from his coworkers and one boss after the next, and had to decide when to speak up and when to be quiet about his faith. He was far from home, and only had a few faithful friends to help keep him accountable. Does that sound a little more relevant?

Actually, the book of Daniel is more about God than it is about Daniel or any of the other characters—how God is in control even though circumstances seem out of control. But it is told from the perspective of stories because God meets us in the nitty-gritty details of life, and telling stories about what happens to us is how we naturally talk to each other. The book of Daniel was written to encourage people who knew that life can throw a lot at you—and it is there that we find relevance to our own lives. The difficulties of our lives do not come as a surprise to God—he has them well in hand, even when we can't quite see how.

The second half of Daniel is less well known and a lot more confusing. Daniel, the interpreter of dreams in the first half of the book, becomes the recipient of dreams, and they're enough to make anyone's knees tremble. They're harder to understand because they're written in a style we're not used to, but fear not! It's well worth plunging in and getting a peek into some of the mysteries that are often beyond our grasp. Even though the style changes from the beginning of the book, the theme remains the same—God is in control even though circumstances seem out of control—and in that message is a great hope.

One remarkable thing about Daniel is how the message points ahead to Christ, even though it was written centuries earlier. We often treat books of the Bible as separate entities, but they are part of one unified story about God. So the themes found in Daniel reach back to the early parts of the Bible, as well as forward to the time of Christ and later. It's no accident that a Christlike figure appears in the fiery furnace, or that the description of Daniel in the lions' den can bring to mind Christ's own tomb. There are still questions that remain about who wrote the book of Daniel and when, but it is clear that a divine author orchestrated a message consistent with God's bigger story that cuts through to our hearts today.

The book of Daniel takes place during the exile. The glory of the kingdom of Israel was brief, followed by a divided kingdom led by an assortment of good and bad kings. The northern kingdom of Israel fell first, taken over by Assyria at the dusk of its power. Then Babylon arose, pushing Egyptian power out of the region and crippling Judah. Daniel was a political hostage, brought to live in Babylon. Eventually Judah fell and the people were scattered, but Daniel remained in Babylon straight through to the time of the next power broker: Persia. Crazy circumstances? Perhaps. But while world powers rose and fell, God was in control and Daniel remained faithful under pressure.

NOTE

1. This section is based on *The NIV Application Commentary: Daniel* (hereafter referred to as *NIVAC: Daniel*) by Tremper Longman III (Grand Rapids: Zondervan, 1999), 19–29.

WHO'S IN CHARGE?

Daniel 1:1–21

I n an important election year, our interest in leaders often rises
a few notches. How have things been going with the country? What needs to change? Who has the best plan to address
the problems of the nation? Post-election results are frequently
different from pre-election hype, as the nation settles down to
watch the test of time. Most interesting, I think, is looking back.
The longer our perspective, the more objectively we can assess
a leader's tenure and evaluate how the complex combination of
circumstances worked together to become history. That longer
perspective can also give us insight into what God is doing in the
world, if we have the eyes to see it that way. More than two and
a half millennia certainly gives us perspective on Babylon—and
the author of Daniel helps us to view it through God's eyes.

A KING WITH GREAT PLANS[1]

Read Daniel 1:1 – 7.

1. What actions by King Nebuchadnezzar demonstrate his dominance over Judah? How might his interest in the youths of Israel further his plans?

2. Put yourself in the shoes of Daniel and his friends. What might you consider to be the pros and cons of living in the king's palace?

3. What indication does the narrator of Daniel give that there might be more powerful forces at work than the might of the Babylonians (1:2)?

GOING DEEPER

The narrator rips away the curtain and informs his readers of the reality behind the appearance. He does so simply by saying that "the Lord delivered Jehoiakim king of Judah into his [Nebuchadnezzar's] hand." Nebuchadnezzar's might, though considerable, was not the reason why Jerusalem fell under his influence; it was the result of the will and action of God himself. This subtle phrase introduces a major theme of the book, the conflict between overweening human power and the power of God.[2]

A KING WITH GRANDER PLANS[3]

Read Daniel 1:8–21.

At this point, we often look to Daniel as an incredible example of faith, who insisted on following his Jewish customs despite the pressures of being in exile, living far away from home in Babylon. While this might be true, it's worth taking a closer look before we leap to conclusions about what that might mean for us today.

4.   Think again about Daniel's experience in the king's palace. What aspects of his life there would compromise his Jewish beliefs? What aspects wouldn't matter? (See for example Deut. 12:20–25; 12:26–28; 16:16–17; 18:9–13; Num. 6:1–4.) In light of this, why might Daniel's focus on food and wine be surprising? What else might you expect him to object to?

5.   Besides simple obedience, what was the primary intent of following God's laws? Does Daniel's plan follow the spirit of the law? Explain.

6.   What explanation can we infer from Daniel and his friends' good health? What is the source of their knowledge and understanding of their Babylonian "curriculum" (1:17)? What does this say about who's in control of this situation?

7. The Jewish exile from Judah began when Nebuchadnezzar took over Jerusalem (605 BC) and ended when Cyrus (the Persian) took over from Nebuchadnezzar's son Belshazzar (539 BC). Daniel 1 points to that entire period in the way it starts and ends. King Nebuchadnezzar's plan was to influence young Israelites for use in the service of the Babylonian kingdom. How does God turn these plans around for his own purposes?

8. Daniel's story is reminiscent of Joseph's story in Genesis 39–41. Skim through Joseph's story. What parallels do you see? How would this and the rest of Daniel 1 be encouraging to the Israelites in exile?

GOING DEEPER

As we read the account of Daniel in the Babylonian and, later, the Persian courts, we must acknowledge [an] important element of discontinuity with our moment in redemptive history. Daniel and his friends lived their lives of faith at a time when God's people were defined as an ethnic group and a distinct political entity. In a word, God's people were a nation, admittedly at the time of Daniel a nation without independent existence, but a nation nonetheless. After Christ, God's people can no longer be so identified. God's people today are the church. A much less tangible entity than a nation, the church spans ethnic, political, and national boundaries.[4]

9. Given the fact that we live in a nation that is not unified by its religion, and live as a religion not bound as a nation, what similarities do Christians face to the circumstances of Daniel in Babylon?

10. On first read, many people are inclined to think that the lesson of Daniel is simply to imitate him. He lived out his faith despite the pressures of living in a different environment from Israel, and stuck to his guns — and so should we. However, as we saw in question 4, that was not the case — in fact it was impossible for Daniel to obey most of the laws of an Israelite. Looking over the chapter again, what kinds of strategies did Daniel use to live wisely within the constraints of his circumstances?

11. What pressures do Christians face today in a multicultural environment? What strategies do we typically employ to cope with the pressure?

12. How does Daniel's example point ahead to Christ's teachings about how to live as Christians in a hostile environment (see Matt. 10:16; John 17:15 – 16; Phil. 3:17 – 20; 1 Peter 2:11 – 12)?

GOING DEEPER

We are to be innocent and shrewd as we live out the issues of faith in our culture. And does this not describe Daniel perfectly? Daniel certainly was innocent. He mounted no angry assault on his captors; rather, he acted quite civilly. He was virtually serpent-like in his crafty strategy to remain faithful in a land antithetical to his deeply held faith. As the story continues, we will observe that Daniel not only remained faithful but exercised significant influence on the godless world around him.[5]

RESPONDING TO GOD'S WORD

IN YOUR GROUP:

There's strength in numbers! Abstaining from the food from the king's table was probably easier because four young men did it together. As a group, think of a service project you can do together before the end of this study that will mark you as Christians working together to make a difference in the world. Designate someone in your group to gather any necessary information you might need to get it on the calendar and make it happen! Pray that you would see God's distinctive work in and through you as a result of the project you take on.

ON YOUR OWN:

Make a list of the pressures you feel most acutely living as a Christian in your particular world. Choose one and think about a strategy that would help you respond differently. Should it be public or private? How does it require a step of faith on your part? How will it help you to see God at work in you? Share your strategy with a friend who can help to keep you accountable.

NOTES

1. This section is based on *NIVAC: Daniel*, 41–51.
2. Longman, 46.
3. This section is based on *NIVAC: Daniel*, 51–69.
4. Longman, 61.
5. Longman, 69.

TRUE
WISDOM

Daniel 2:1–49

I f my dreams are anything to go by, they're not exactly a resource for any great wisdom! They do reveal something about my hopes and fears, the things I've been thinking about lately, or the circumstances that have surrounded me. But if I were a betting person, I certainly wouldn't suggest putting any money on them for predicting the future! That's not to say that God couldn't still speak through dreams if he wanted to. But at this time, in my culture at least, it isn't the norm. Not so in Babylon back in Daniel's day. Dreams were big business — magicians, enchanters, sorcerers, and astrologers could actually make a living off of dreams; people spent years studying the right indicators to interpret them correctly. There was much higher regard for dreams then, even across cultures — a point of contact for Jews and Babylonians alike, even if they relied on different sources for interpretation.

SEARCHING FOR WISDOM[1]

Read Daniel 2:1–23.

1. What is unusual about King Nebuchadnezzar's request for an interpretation of his dream? How can you tell it is unusual, even in the Babylonian culture?

2. The king's wise men declare, "What the king asks is too difficult. No one can reveal [the dream] to the king except the gods, and they do not live among human beings" (2:11). Does Daniel agree (see 2:27–28)? How does Daniel demonstrate wisdom in the way he approaches this problem?

 The Babylonian sages were only half right. While no human being could ever tell the king the contents and interpretation of his dream, God can, and, in contrast to the beliefs of the Babylonians (2:11), there is a God who lives among people: Daniel's God.[2]

GOING DEEPER

3. Daniel 2 presents a contest of sorts: Daniel versus the Babylonian advisers. But underlying that contest are deeper issues. What is really at stake here? How does the situation in Daniel 2 raise the bar on Daniel's wisdom compared to Daniel 1?

4. What do we learn about God through Daniel's interactions with him in this part of the chapter, as well as from Daniel's response of praise in 2:20–23?

5. Wisdom is a big theme throughout Scripture. What do the following verses, from the books that "major" on wisdom, have in common with what we're learning about wisdom in Daniel?

Proverbs 1:1–7

Job 28:12–28

Ecclesiates 12:13–14

6. How does Daniel 2 continue to develop themes found in Daniel 1? How would it have encouraged the exiles? How does it encourage you?

We must not let our curiosity concerning God's revelation of future events distract us from the main theme of the chapter: *Only God's wisdom can reveal the mysteries of life.* In other words, it is not the content of the revelation of the future that is primary; what is most important here is the fact that it is only Daniel's God that knows that future.[3]

RESPONDING TO WISDOM[4]

Read Daniel 2:24–49.

7. Judging from the response of King Nebuchadnezzar (2:46–47), Daniel got the dream and its interpretation right on. What impact does this have on the lives of Daniel and his friends? On the Babylonian wise men? On King Nebuchadnezzar?

8. King Nebuchadnezzar, one of the world's most powerful leaders, falls prostrate before Daniel, an exiled Jew and servant to the Babylonian kingdom. Once again, the wisdom of Babylon is shown up by the wisdom of God. Compare the language of 2:37–38 and 2:46 with 1 Timothy 6:13–16 and Revelation 19:11–16. How does King Nebuchadnezzar reflect the glory of God? How does he represent a counterfeit?

9. There are two major interpretations as to which four rising powers Nebu-chadnezzar's dream corresponds to historically: either Babylon–Medo/Persians–Greeks–Romans, or Babylon–Medes–Persians–Greeks. Regardless of how this plays out in the details, what general characteristics can you determine from the symbolism in the dream—both the materials of the statue, and the rock that overtakes it?

GOING DEEPER

In the light of this interpretive confusion, we must entertain seriously the idea that the vision of Daniel 2 does not intend to be precise as it writes its history before it occurs. In other words, though it starts in the concrete present, it is a wrong strategy to proceed through history and associate the different stages of the statue with particular empires. The vision intends to communicate something more general, but also more grand: God is sovereign; he is in control despite present conditions.[5]

10. It might have been hard for Daniel to imagine "a kingdom that will never be destroyed" (2:44), having lived through the takeover of his beloved country by the Babylonians. But today we have a very different vantage point. Compare the language of Luke 20:17–18 with the language of Daniel 2. What (or who) is the rock Daniel refers to? How is the kingdom that emerges different from what anyone would have imagined, even in New Testament times?

11. When Daniel praised God for revealing Nebuchadnezzar's dream to him, he said, "Praise be to the name of God forever and ever; wisdom and power are his" (2:20). The New Testament gets more specific than the Old Testament about finding wisdom. Read 1 Corinthians 1:20–25. What does the wisdom and power of God look like in this passage? How do we get hold of it? How does Nebuchadnezzar's response to Daniel point ahead to this idea?

12. From Genesis to Revelation, the Bible consistently points to the understanding that wisdom is found through a relationship with God, not through the discoveries or philosophies of humankind apart from God. Read Colossians 2:1–10. How can we grow in true wisdom?

GOING DEEPER

We live in an increasingly complex and confusing world. With every new and improved technological advance, we are told that our lives will be simpler and easier. That's the hype, but when we buy our computer, log onto the Internet, or get our cellular phone, we find a whole host of new questions and obstacles facing us there. Where will we find the wisdom necessary to live in a world of growing complexity? Many think it is through intelligence, which we often confuse with wisdom.... Biblical wisdom is more than a knowledge of facts, it is more like a skill (a "knowing how" rather than a "knowing that") based on our relationship with Jesus Christ. Wisdom is a divinely given ability to have insight as to the best way to live life.[6]

RESPONDING TO GOD'S WORD

IN YOUR GROUP:

We can grow in wisdom because we have a God who lives among us. Consider people and circumstances that have "lived among you." Take some time to share in your group how these individuals or events impacted your life. For example, a new baby, a new roommate, or an aging parent moving in will change your schedule, how you think, and what you do from day to day. A new exercise routine, a diet, or an illness can "live among you" and change your perceptions. Discuss what it would take for God, "living among you," to similarly change your day-to-day lives.

ON YOUR OWN:

Read Psalm 118, from which the phrase referring to Jesus as a rock, or stone, is quoted in numerous New Testament accounts (Ps. 118:22). As you read it, picture yourself in Daniel's shoes, after God enabled him to interpret King Nebuchadnezzar's dream. Then read it again from your own perspective, knowing Christ to be the salvation that God provided for us.

NOTES

1. This section is based on *NIVAC: Daniel*, 70–79 and 84–87.
2. Longman, 78.
3. Longman, 73.
4. This section is based on *NIVAC: Daniel*, 79–84 and 87–93.
5. Longman, 82.
6. Longman, 90, 91.

SAVING
POWER

Daniel 3:1–30

What's your greatest fear? Public speaking? Drowning? Heights? Being the laughing stock in a crowd? Many people spend a lot of time and anxious thoughts wondering how they would behave in their worst-case scenario. The truth is, worrying about what's in the future is often much worse than dealing with the moment when—and if—it actually arrives. Somehow, in the heat of the moment, we are often given the grace to deal with things we could never imagine dealing with under normal conditions. I can't imagine what it would be like to face a fiery furnace as punishment for not bowing down to and worshiping a statue. Would my faith stand the test? Would I rationalize and hope for God's forgiveness? I honestly don't know—but that's not likely to be the test of my life. I'm better off learning from those who did prove faithful, and more importantly, leaning on the One who met them in their crisis, and trust that the saving power that delivered them is with me as well.

THE HEART OF THE MATTER[1]

Read Daniel 3:1 – 15.

1. When a phrase is used once, we try to understand what it means. But when a phrase is repeated two, three, even six times, that's an attention-getter! What phrases do you notice being repeated in 3:1 – 15? What do you think the author is trying to emphasize?

2. By now, we're getting a sense of what sort of person King Nebuchadnezzar is. What is your overall impression of him? What would it be like to live in his empire?

3. The day starts out well for Nebuchadnezzar. His ninety-foot-high statue is complete, and he's got virtually his whole kingdom trained to fall down at the sound of the music. What is at the heart of the people's worship? What do you think is motivating the astrologers (3:8 – 12)? What is most important to the king about all this?

4. The literary tension mounts as Nebuchadnezzar confronts Shadrach, Meshach, and Abednego. He brings up the music motif one more time—will they fall down in worship according to the king's specifications, or won't they (3:15)? It's a court conflict that's bound to have dire consequences. What question is at the root of the conflict (3:15)? How does the history of the Jews enable Shadrach, Meshach, and Abednego to give an informed answer to the king (if they have the guts to do it)?

GOING DEEPER

In chapter 2, God made known his great wisdom. Here, he will reveal his power. The story in this way will again support the overarching theme of the book of Daniel: *In spite of present appearances, God is in control.* The specific focus of this chapter is that God's power transcends even death. This stirring story intends to bolster the courage of God's people as they face what seems to be overwhelming odds.[2]

5. This story may seem a far cry from our reality. Unless you happen to live somewhere under an oppressive government, bowing down to some huge image isn't generally a real threat we have to face. But bowing down to someone else's will, or being motivated to put our own self-interests first—that sort of worship comes closer to home. What are the things that tend to make you happy and satisfied? Who or what is behind what drives your day-to-day interactions?

The list [of idols] is vast, which is why the danger is so real. The seduction is subtle, which is why we can slip so easily into idol worship. But though subtle and varied, I suggest that idolatry, whether of Nebuchadnezzar's sort or the kind we discover in our own hearts, ultimately has one object. When the masks are ripped away, behind every idol is the *self*.[3]

6. Everything would have been fine for Shadrach, Meshach, and Abednego if it hadn't been for the astrologers calling attention to them. What sort of things call attention to you as a Christian and put your faith on the line? Is this good or bad? How do such things influence your faith?

A MIRACULOUS DELIVERANCE[4]

Read Daniel 3:16–30.

7. How does Shadrach, Meshach, and Abednego's response to Nebuchadnezzar reveal the depth of their faith? Is their faith dependent on God's answer as to whether they live or die? What can we learn from them?

8. How does the author's attention to details add to the story's impact (see, for example, 3:19–23, 26–27)?

9. God's miraculous deliverance turns the tables on those who were denouncing Shadrach, Meshach, and Abednego. How is the king's opinion changed? What becomes of the three young men? What will become of the power-hungry astrologers if they continue to oppose the Jews (3:29)?

GOING DEEPER

Loyalty to a godless and foolish king brings death, not the life one would expect.... By contrast, it is only the true God who can proclaim that "no one can deliver out of my hand" (Deut. 32:39). And this great God was a proven deliverer. After all, when he rescued his people from Egypt centuries before, Moses told the Israelites that it was God who "brought you out of the iron-smelting furnace, out of Egypt, to be the people of his inheritance, as you now are" (Deut. 4:20).[5]

10. There's a lot of speculation and mystery surrounding the fourth person in the furnace. The description by a pagan king—"a son of the gods" (3:25) or "an angel" (3:28)—is not necessarily reliable.[6] What can we undeniably say about the deliverance of Shadrach, Meshach, and Abednego? What

was the impact on Nebuchadnezzar and his satraps, prefects, governors, and royal advisers (3:27–28)?

GOING DEEPER

[The great Reformation theologian John] Calvin pointed out that if God wanted, he could have extinguished the flames of the fire in order to save the three men. He saved them *in* the fire, not *from* the fire. They were in the very jaws of death. Moreover, he could have saved them without further fanfare, simply having them walk out of the fire unscathed, but instead he chose to save them by the presence of a "fourth [who] looks like a son of the gods" (v. 25).... God dwelt with the three friends in the midst of the flames to preserve them from harm. In this sense, the Christian cannot help but see a prefigurement of Jesus Christ, who came to earth to dwell in a chaotic world and who even experienced death, not so that we might escape the experience of death but that we might have victory over it.[7]

11. We can be quick to doubt God's presence when the going gets rough: *How could this happen to me? Where was God when ... ? How can I believe in a God who allows ... ?* What does this story teach us about suffering? What impact do you think it had on Shadrach, Meshach, and Abednego?

12. We live in a time when many people are rather dubious of miracles. Has God's influence in this world changed in character since the time of Daniel and his friends? What do we learn from Ephesians 1:18–21 regarding God's power?

RESPONDING TO GOD'S WORD

IN YOUR GROUP:

Share about a time that you may have dreaded, and how dealing with it was different from your anticipation of it when it actually arrived. Or share about a crisis that you never would have anticipated, but you performed better than you could have imagined.

ON YOUR OWN:

Think about the idols in your life from question 5 — the things that drive your day-to-day interactions and define your happiness. How will your life be different if they are taken away for some uncontrollable reason? Reflect on how these idols are different from the power of the Most High God, who dwells with us through all circumstances. Take some time to worship the God who is with you, right at this moment, closer than you can even imagine.

NOTES

1. This section is based on *NIVAC: Daniel*, 94–100, 103–106, and 109–111.
2. Longman, 97, italics original.
3. Longman, 109–110, italics original.
4. This section is based on *NIVAC: Daniel*, 100–103, 107–109, and 111–112.
5. Longman, 102.
6. Longman, 103.
7. Longman, 111–112, italics original.

PRIDE GOES
BEFORE A FALL

Daniel 4:1–37

Have you ever thought about the number of sayings associated with the fall that comes from pride? Could it be that it's a very common human predicament? How often have you heard, "Pride goeth before a fall"? Are you the kind of person who relishes the fall of the proud, or do you feel bad when "another one bites the dust"? It might depend a bit on your own experience. It's never an easy thing to admit you're wrong, but "the bigger they come, the harder they fall." Perhaps no fall from pride ever recorded is greater than that of King Nebuchadnezzar of Babylon. He himself observes, "Those who walk in pride [God] is able to humble" (Dan. 4:37b).

AN UNEXPECTED TURN OF EVENTS[1]

Read Daniel 4:1–37.

1. This chapter opens and closes with first-person language—the king himself speaks! Do his statements (4:1–3, 34–35) take you by surprise? Explain. What impact, if any, would they have on the king's subjects?

2. Does this sound like the same king we've met in the first three chapters of Daniel? How do Nebuchadnezzar's opening and closing doxologies contrast to what we've seen so far of him, as well as the Nebuchadnezzar we see in 4:4–5, 29–30?

3. It seems a bit mysterious that all the wise men of Babylon could not interpret the king's dream. What dynamics beyond mere knowledge might be at work?

4. We're left in the dark about the king's reaction to Daniel. Instead, the author fast-forwards a year to the fulfillment of the dream. In the continuing contest for who is the most powerful god, how does the Most High teach Nebuchadnezzar a lesson he's not likely to forget anytime soon? How is it different from earlier lessons?

"A man who thinks he is like a god must become a beast to learn that he is only a human being."[2]

5. Consider Daniel's advice to the king (4:27) compared to the lesson Nebuchadnezzar learned through seven years of hardship. Which was a more effective teacher? Is this consistent with your own life experience? Is one way preferable to the other?

6. Keep in mind that the message of Daniel was written for the benefit of the exiles. How would this chapter be an encouragement to them?

AN ALL-TOO-FAMILIAR STORY[3]

GOING DEEPER

This use of the tree as an image of the life-giving nature of the king has previously been used in biblical tradition (cf. Ezek. 17:1–10; 31:3–14 ...). The story also connects with the ancient Near East. There is little about a "sacred" or "cosmic" tree in the literature of Mesopotamia, but the tree occurs as a major motif in the iconography.... [I]f the Tree symbolized the divine world order, then the king himself represented the realization of that order in man, in other words, a true image of God, the Perfect Man.[4]

7. A very similar tree to Nebuchadnezzar's dream-tree is described in Ezekiel, there referring to the earlier empire of Assyria. Read Ezekiel 31:3 – 14. What made this tree great? What was its "crime"?

Did your mind start thinking about the tree of life in Genesis when you read Ezekiel? It should! Patterns like this in God's Word are meant to help you connect to big themes that pop up consistently. Following the trail of related images should help you find meaning that goes beyond one particularly proud, powerful king in a particularly powerful kingdom at a specific point of time in history — meaning that can apply to all people at all times.

8. Genesis 2, viewed from the perspective of ancient Near Eastern culture, which would have been familiar to the original readers, evokes the image of God as a successful king over heaven and earth, looking over his dwelling place. Having an extensive garden with a great variety of fruit and shade trees, watercourses, pools, and paths is a sign that this king has influence over a vast area and now enjoys a time of peace and prosperity.[5] The man he created is his chosen servant to work and care for his garden. How does this way of viewing Genesis 2 compare to Daniel 4:29 – 30? What is similar? What is different?

9. How does God's servant in Genesis 2 take things into his own hands in Genesis 3? What are the consequences? Any parallels here to King Nebuchadnezzar?

10. Genesis 3 is not the only time humanity has tried to push its limits. Read Genesis 11:1–9. What patterns do you see developing in the relationships between God and people? How does the tower of Babel connect particularly to King Nebuchadnezzar's situation?

11. Let's jump ahead from Genesis 11 to the Psalms, at a time and place we would expect to find belief and trust in God, rather than a competitive thrust against him. Read Psalm 73:1–14. How does the psalmist's attitude in verses 2–14 contradict his statement in verse 1? What is at the root of his longings? What are the consequences of his attitude (vv. 21–22)? Can you identify with the psalmist's struggle?

12. So where do we turn to for hope if, as human beings, we struggle endlessly with hearts that tend to our own ways rather than to God's kingdom? Isaiah, who lived a bit before the time of Daniel, also refers to a tree similar to Nebuchadnezzar's dream-tree. Read Isaiah 10:33–11:3. What part of Isaiah's prophecy is similar to Nebuchadnezzar's dream? Where does the focus shift? How does Isaiah's prophecy point to hope for all of humankind?

GOING DEEPER

Our God is a God who turns shame into rejoicing. But he does not do this by some sort of magical fiat. The gospel story is the story of God himself experiencing shame on our behalf. He subjected himself to the humiliation of the cross. Christ felt shame, but he underwent the experience in order to free us from shame and invite us to the glory of the resurrection.[6]

RESPONDING TO GOD'S WORD

IN YOUR GROUP:

"Pride, in the negative sense, is a conception of one's self-worth that exceeds the bounds of propriety."[7] It's easy to see that King Nebuchadnezzar exceeded those bounds. As a group, discuss what those bounds of propriety look like in "normal" people. Are you guilty of an unhealthy pride?

ON YOUR OWN:

If dreams could really come true, what would be the top ten ways you would spend a day? Make a list, just for fun!

In Psalm 84:10, the psalmist declares, "Better is one day in [God's] courts than a thousand elsewhere." Do you believe this? In your heart of hearts, how do your top ten days compare to the psalmist's declaration?

NOTES

1. This section is based on *NIVAC: Daniel*, 113–122.
2. D. N. Fewell, *Circle of Sovereignty: A Story of Stories in Daniel 1–6*, Journal for the Study of the Old Testament, Supplement 72 (Sheffield, England: JSOT, 1988), 101, quoted in Longman, 122.
3. This section is based on *NIVAC: Daniel*, 123–130.
4. Longman, 119.
5. *The NIV Application Commentary: Genesis*, by John H. Walton (Grand Rapids: Zondervan, 2001), 166–167.
6. Longman, 129–130.
7. Longman, 123.

WEIGHING IN

Daniel 5:1–31

There are all sorts of standards that we use to gauge our progress in all manner of things. What would a weight-loss program be without weighing in? What student doesn't want to know how he or she fared compared to the standard? We have scales for temperature, scales for pain, scales for talent, for structural stability, for salaries, for intelligence, and on and on. We need standards to figure out if we're acting within certain limits, or if we need to adjust things for safety, health, or well-being. Sometimes we use standards inappropriately—to compare one person with another—and get caught up in making unnecessary judgments. But ultimately, our standards point to a God who cares about what each of us does. We will be measured by his standards, for better or for worse.

DÉJÀ VU[1]

Read Daniel 5:1–17.

1. Although this chapter stands on its own as another incident in Daniel's life, it's hard not to notice similarities to what's already happened. What elements of the story do you notice from previous chapters (5:2, 6, 7–8, 17)?

2. What are the most significant differences from previous chapters (5:1, 5, 10, 17)?

GOING DEEPER

The main character of Daniel 5 is Belshazzar ... whose presence in the narrative raises interesting and difficult historical questions ... since the rather full extrabiblical accounts of the lineage of neo-Babylonian kings make no mention of a king called Belshazzar. After the death of Nebuchadnezzar in 562 BC, he was succeeded by [four generations of kings]. Nabonidus is recorded as the last king of the Babylonians, since he ruled until the time Cyrus entered Babylon and brought his kingdom to an end (539 BC).... Until recently Belshazzar was thought to be one of those errors in the Bible's understanding of history that led many to doubt its accuracy.... Today we have abundant textual witness to the fact that he was the son of Nabonidus. More than that, Belshazzar was coregent and actually in charge of Babylon during his father's ten-year absence from the capital city, thus explaining the reference to him as king.[2]

3. Nebuchadnezzar and Belshazzar were both powerful Babylonian kings. What similarities do you see in them? What is different?

GOING DEEPER

A close reading of the text reveals a condescending attitude by Belshazzar toward [Daniel] who played such a significant role in Nebuchadnezzar's life.... The king first identifies him as one of the captives: "Are you Daniel, one of the exiles my father the king brought from Judah?" (v. 13). Such an address intends to remind Daniel of his place before Belshazzar. Belshazzar is king; Daniel is his captive. Calvin understood the tone of the king's speech when he states that "the king does not acknowledge his negligence but interrogates Daniel without shame—and interrogates him as if he were a prisoner."

Belshazzar then launches off a series of honorifics that cite Daniel's abilities and character, but again a close reading of the speech shows that the king himself does not endorse the reports.[3]

NIGHT FALLS ON BABYLON[4]

Read Daniel 5:18–31.

4. Do you think Daniel's response to Belshazzar is influenced by Belshazzar's attitude toward Daniel? Explain, giving examples from the text. How are your interactions influenced by the attitudes of others toward you (whether real or perceived)?

5. Imagine a hand actually writing on the wall! The fact that others saw it besides the king proves it was not just a hallucination. In fact, excavations support the fact that the walls were coated with white gypsum, which would allow the writing to be clearly seen.[5] Think about the imagery: The God who *holds in his hand* your life (5:23) is the same God who *sent the hand* to write the inscription (5:24). Job expressed a similar sentiment when he said, "The LORD gave, and the LORD has taken away; may the name of the LORD be praised" (Job 1:21). How does Belshazzar reflect a different worldview? Which position is a better reflection of the way you live your life?

6. Daniel's Hebrew name means "God is my judge." His Babylonian name, Belteshazzar, means "May [a god] protect his life" or "Lady [a goddess], protect the king."[6] Compare the use of Daniel's names in Daniel 4 and 5. How does the use of his name reflect Daniel's different roles in the kings' lives? How does this mirror different aspects of God's character? Are they contradictory?

7. Why do you suppose Belshazzar is given such a sudden, final judgment compared to Nebuchadnezzar, who had numerous warnings, and then

seven years of wandering like a beast before he humbled himself before God and was restored (5:22)?

8. How do you measure up? The concept of scales and weighing, associated with judgment, is common to nearly all religions, including Christianity. When your final day comes, will the good outweigh the bad? Will you be "found wanting" (5:27) like Belshazzar? Does your own "weighing in" fill you with fear or confidence? Explain.

9. How does the Bible regard God's justice (see Ps. 67:4; 96:13; Prov. 21:15; Mal. 4:1–3)? What makes this possible (see Isa. 51:5; 53:4–6; Rom. 5:6–11; 8:31–34)?

10. In the days of Babylon, a clear distinction existed between things sacred and things common. Items from any god's temple were regarded as holy; if common people were to use them for everyday purposes, it was an abomination that invited judgment.[7] The lines are a bit fuzzier now. There are some exceptions, but for the most part today, anything goes—and each

new generation seems to consider fewer things "sacred." Have things changed? Are the standards for justice any different? Are we off the hook because we think we know better now? What does it look like now, compared to Belshazzar's time, to set ourselves up against the Lord of heaven?

It is not that there is nothing holy, but that *everything is holy*.... Whereas before Christ God made his presence known in a special way in a certain location, today we can meet God anywhere.... Such an understanding intensifies the concept of blasphemy. Blasphemy is not just defacing a church or a cross. It is a misuse of any part of God's creation. An assault against a fellow human being is an act of blasphemy. After all, we are all created in the image of God.... An angry word spoken against a fellow believer is an act of blasphemy. After all, Christians are all temples of the Holy Spirit.... The destruction of the environment for selfish purposes is an act of blasphemy. The land, the air, the seas are each the creation of our holy God.... [W]hen we fully understand blasphemy, we are staggered by the extent to which each and every one of us is implicated.... The world today is far better informed than in the days of Belshazzar. We have been warned and given clear directions about a proper relationship with God. God himself has given the people of the world a direct message through his Word.[8]

11. Daniel makes a very clear judgment against King Belshazzar's excessive pride and attitude against God. To what extent can we act similarly? Take into consideration the following verses:

Matthew 7:1–5

John 9:1–3

Romans 2:1–4

Romans 11:33–36

James 2:8–11

I Infortunately, I would hazard to guess that the Christian community, in the Western world at least, would be characterized by the watching world as narrow, intolerant, judgmental, and self-righteous rather than forgiving, compassionate, gracious, and redemptive. All of us who call on the name of Christ must do some serious soul-searching and repenting as we reach out to transform the world in our Lord's name.[9]

RESPONDING TO GOD'S WORD

IN YOUR GROUP:

Discuss some recent current events that have characterized the Christian community as narrow, intolerant, judgmental, and/or self-righteous. Were the accusations deserved? How do Christians do the same thing toward non-Christians? Discuss how we as Christians can participate in the current climate to make a difference.

ON YOUR OWN:

One scholar has made the observation that the annual rising of Libra (the constellation called the Scales) took place on the eve of Babylon's fall to the Persians, further emphasizing God's "weighing in" of Belshazzar.[10]

Go outside on a dark night, if you can, and take a few minutes to study the stars. Consider the works of God's hands and your place in his universe. Take time to thank God that, as far as the farthest star is, he has removed your sin even further from you by sending his Son, Jesus.

> For as high as the heavens are above the earth,
> so great is his love for those who fear him;
> As far as the east is from the west,
> so far has he removed our transgressions from us. (Ps. 103:11–12)

NOTES

1. This section is based on *NIVAC: Daniel*, 131–140.
2. Longman, 134–135.
3. Longman, 140.
4. This section is based on *NIVAC: Daniel*, 140–154.
5. Longman, 138.
6. Longman, 50.
7. Longman, 152.
8. Longman, 152–153, italics original.
9. Longman, 151.
10. Longman, 142, citing Al Wolters, "The Riddle of the Scales in Daniel 5" *Hebrew Union College Annual* 62 (1991): 155.

PREVAILING LAW

Daniel 6:1–28

Have you ever thought about the unspoken rules that compete for your attention? The classic one, of course, is the secret speed limit. We know the posted speed—but what's the Real Limit that the ones giving the tickets consider too high? A common mistake of young parents is allowing the invisible Law of True Obedience. *Mom or Dad said they'd give me three chances, but what they really meant was when they start screaming and jumping up and down, I'd better listen or else something's going to actually happen.* One of the favorites in my house is the Procrastination Law, which is generally gauged by the amount of panic built up before a deadline—no one ever knows exactly when it will be superseded by the Law of Getting Things Done on Time. The new ruler of Babylon, Darius the Mede, still had much to learn as to the prevailing laws at work in the kingdom.

CONFLICT IN THE COURT ... AGAIN[1]

Read Daniel 6:1–28.

1. This chapter concludes the narrative portion of Daniel's activities in Babylon. Trace Daniel's political career in 1:3–4, 19–20; 2:48–49; 4:9; 5:29; and 6:1–2, 28. What does this

tell you about Daniel? What does it tell you about God and the theme of this book?

2. What parallels do you see between Daniel 6 and previous chapters? In what ways are they different?

3. From what you know of Daniel so far, does his description in 6:1 – 5 surprise you? Read 1 Peter 2:11 – 12. How well does Daniel fit the bill? How well do you? Does Daniel's example make Peter's description seem more doable for you? Explain.

4. Proverbs 28:10 reads, "Those who lead the upright along an evil path will fall into their own trap, but the blameless will receive a good inheritance." Who is leading whom in Daniel 6? What's the result?

5. According to the law of the Medes and Persians, no decree or edict that the king issues can be changed (6:8, 15). What effect does the king's own law have on himself? How does Daniel 6 show evidence of a higher law at work?

Perhaps it is best to consider the lions' den a trial by ordeal rather than an execution per se. An execution, after all, would not have a time limit. The understanding of the scene as an ordeal also explains some of the language found in the chapter. What was an ordeal? An individual was subjected to an ordeal when he was suspected of a crime, but there was some uncertainty as to his guilt. Daniel's guilt in relationship to Darius's decree appears clear, but as he emerges from the den, he claims that the lions have not hurt him "because I was found innocent in [God's] sight. Nor have I ever done any wrong before you, O king" (v. 22). Daniel's survival attests to his innocence.

The theology behind an ordeal is that God, who knows the heart in a way that human judges do not, will see the verdict through. Daniel's survival, then, is God's judgment of innocence on Daniel. In this judgment, Darius rejoices.[2]

A HIGHER LAW[3]

6. Read Psalm 19:7–11. How does God's law compare to man's law, as illustrated by Daniel 6:7–9?

7. Jesus summarized God's law in Matthew 22:37–39 as: "Love the Lord your God with all your heart and with all your soul and with all your mind.... [and] love your neighbor as yourself." Is this consistent with Psalm 19:7–11? If so, why do we have such a hard time obeying it?

8. What effect does the king's law have on Daniel (6:10)? What is the cost of obedience to God's law in the short term for Daniel? In the long term?

GOING DEEPER

Darius, the most powerful human being in the world, has no power to save Daniel. But Daniel's faith is founded on a person who is more powerful than the king, God himself. As events unfold, we observe another important biblical theme in operation: God overrules the evil intentions of human beings to bring about great salvation.[4]

9. As we've seen in other sessions, it's a helpful exercise to look backward and forward in Scripture to learn from similar situations. It helps us understand the Bible's overarching themes and strengthens our picture of God. Read Genesis 39:2–6; 41:15–16, 39–40; 45:4–8; 50:18–20. What parallels do you see between Joseph and Daniel? What does it teach you about their God?

10. Looking ahead in Scripture, read Acts 5:12–21a, 27–32 (or 5:12–42 if you have more time). What similarities do you see between Daniel and the apostles? What does it teach you about their God?

11. How does Daniel's ordeal point ahead to Jesus himself (6:17–23)? What is different about their ordeals?

GOING DEEPER

The modern parallels to Daniel 6 in Western democracies take place not in the arena of culture wars, but rather in more local situations. A librarian is fired because she refuses to work on a Sunday morning during worship services. A young teenager is told by his parents that he may not meet with the neighborhood church's youth group for prayer because they do not want him involved in "all that superstition." A wife is told that she can be a Christian, but must not act like it around the house. Where we today most often encounter conflict analogous to Daniel 6 is the law of God versus the law of an employer, a parent, a spouse.[5]

12. What circumstances do you face that require the quiet faithfulness of Daniel—faithfulness that doesn't attempt open rebellion to an authority figure, but quietly continues to worship God, "just as [you] had done

before" (6:10) — faithfulness that believes that the law of God will bring joy to the heart more than will bowing down to the laws of others?

RESPONDING TO GOD'S WORD

IN YOUR GROUP:

There is no one more powerful than Jesus, who has saved us from eternal death. However, God makes use of various means to protect us on this earth as well. Share experiences with your group where you felt a sense of God's presence protecting you from very present danger. When you are done, recite together Darius's closing words (Dan. 6:26–27), personalized here:

> *For he is the living God*
> *and he endures forever;*
> *his kingdom will not be destroyed,*
> *his dominion will never end.*
> *He rescues and he saves;*
> *he performs signs and wonders*
> *in the heavens and on the earth.*
> *He has rescued me*
> *from the power of death itself.*

ON YOUR OWN:

Treat yourself to a dessert today! While you're enjoying it, read Psalm 19:7–11 again and reflect on the sweetness of God's law. Every time you have something sweet this week, think about ways in which God's law is refreshing, trustworthy, and joyful.

NOTES

1. This section is based on *NIVAC: Daniel*, 155–166.
2. Longman, 162–163.
3. This section is based on *NIVAC: Daniel*, 166–173.
4. Longman, 168.
5. Longman, 171.

THE HORROR OF HUMAN EVIL

Daniel 7:1–28

In general, I expect movies to be entertaining. Different people certainly have different views on what constitutes entertainment—drama, action, comedy, suspense, romance, to name a few. But every now and then I come across movies that are compelling for other reasons. They leave me with a sick feeling in the pit of my stomach as I am reminded of the depth of human evil. Horrible images remain in my mind, making me want to weep over just how bad people can really be—how much suffering they can inflict on others. I believe the first such movie for me was *The Killing Fields*, documenting the horror of the Khmer Rouge in Cambodia. We like to think the best of human nature, and everyone loves a happy ending. But reality points to the fact that unrestrained human nature is actually worse than most of us can even imagine. Daniel is given a glimpse of the horror of human evil in a dream, the first of several visions that give him a sketchy image of the world's future.

DANIEL'S DREAM[1]

Read Daniel 7:1 – 14.

1. Although we've dealt with dreams before in Daniel, chapter 7 clearly takes us in a different direction from the stories of Daniel's life in the Babylonian court. There's a complete switch in genre (the style of literature) from court narrative to apocalypse. What's different from the previous chapters? What's confusing? What's the overall impression you get from the story line?

GOING DEEPER

[A]pocalyptic is a metaphor-rich genre. In this regard it is like poetry. Metaphors and similes teach by analogy. They throw light on difficult concepts and things by relating them to something we know from common experience. As such, images speak truly and accurately, but not precisely. We often do not know where the analogy stops. In this way, images preserve mystery about ideas that are ultimately beyond our comprehension. It is a travesty, then, to interpret apocalyptic images too finely, to press them in their details. As we will see, this mistake is common among biblical interpreters of apocalyptic and has led to all kinds of fanciful interpretations and outlandish claims. Caution and reserve are virtues in the interpretation of apocalyptic.[2]

2. So how do we begin to understand the metaphors? We have to connect as best as possible to whatever our own common experiences suggest. But more importantly, we need to understand a bit of Near Eastern context to make sense of the images — through biblical literature as well as outside sources. In 7:2 – 3, what is your own impression of the great sea?

What do the following verses say about how the sea was regarded in biblical times?

Job 7:12

Job 38:8 – 11

Isaiah 17:12

Jeremiah 5:22

Revelation 21:1

GOING DEEPER

The most well-known creation story of the Babylonians is the *Enuma Elish*. This tale begins with an account of the creation of the gods ... [that] relates the creation of the world in the light of the struggle between the Creator and the Sea....

[D]eep in the psyche of the people of the ancient Near East the sea was more than a dangerous place. It was a threatening force that ranged against the beneficial forces of creation.[3]

3. Out of this foreboding sea come four beasts. You don't have to be able to picture all the details exactly to get a sense of what they're like. Would you want to be there when they come out of the sea? What details help you characterize the beasts? Who is their enemy?

4. Now let's look at the beasts in a more biblical context. Read Genesis 1:21, 24–26 and Deuteronomy 22:9–11. Note the importance of the separation of kinds in the order of creation. In what ways do the beasts (like the great sea they came from) demonstrate a threat against God's created world? In what ways do they threaten God's order in creation?

GOING DEEPER

[The beasts] are symbols of forces ranged against God and his creation order. These beasts are bizarre; they are mutants, perversions of what God intended by his creation. As such, they evoke not only horror in the original reader, but also revulsion.[4]

5. Suddenly the scene changes to a courtroom. Think about all the images and metaphors in 7:9–14 first from your own perspective. What do they mean to you? Who is the clear victor?

6. How does the imagery of the Ancient of Days and son of man tie in with Old Testament understanding (see Gen. 1:27; Ex. 13:21; 19:16; Ps. 68:4; 104:3 – 4)? What would this imagery in Daniel 7 mean to the original audience?

GOING DEEPER

Like the sea image, the motif of God riding clouds also has an ancient Near Eastern background.... Baal, the chief deity and primary divine warrior of that culture, is often called the "Rider on the Clouds." ... Baal was the god of the thunderstorm in the Ugaritic pantheon. His cloud-riding was appropriate to his function....

The vision [in Daniel 7:1 – 14] is more than descriptive of these two realms: human evil and divine judgment. It also narrates a conflict between the two, with a certain and clear conclusion.... In a word, though human evil thrives in the present, God is in control and will have the final victory.[5]

UNDERSTANDING THE DREAM[6]

Read Daniel 7:15 – 28.

7. Can you relate to Daniel being troubled and disturbed by his vision (7:15)? Who does he turn to for help in understanding his dream (7:16)? What does the answer add to your understanding (7:17, 23 – 27)?

8. In what respect is the conclusion of the dream hopeful? How is it disturbing?

9. Daniel gets a glimpse into the horror of human evil that is portrayed by the beasts. But before we start pointing fingers at the leaders of these kingdoms, consider Paul's argument in the beginning of Romans. The first chapter points out the wrath of God against human beings generally (Rom. 1:18). The second chapter switches to Jews who might be pointing the finger at the people in chapter one, and condemns them too (Rom. 2:1). What is Paul's conclusion in Romans 3:10–18 (pulling from a variety of Old Testament references)?

10. How is "corporate sin" worse than individual sin? What examples do you see around you on a regular basis? What kinds of corporate sin do you participate in?

11. Before you get on a bandwagon to fight against your pet "corporate sin" group, read Ephesians 6:12–20. How does Paul's vision of the battle against evil add to Daniel's vision? What or who are we fighting against? What means do we have to participate in the battle?

12. Read Revelation 13:1–10. How is John's vision of the battle against evil in the book of Revelation consistent with Daniel's vision? Are the conclusions of Daniel (7:18), Paul (Eph. 6:14a), and John (Rev. 13:10b) consistent? Explain. What hope do we have that we will be counted among the faithful saints and not siding with the beast when the Son of Man comes with the clouds (Rev. 1.4–7)?

GOING DEEPER

From the beginning of the canon ... to its end in Revelation, God's people are told that their Lord fights for them against the evil that oppresses them—both external enemies and the sin that remains in our own hearts.... God has won the victory on the cross, and history's victorious denouement is certain.[9]

RESPONDING TO GOD'S WORD

IN YOUR GROUP:

What movies come to mind when you think of "the horror of human evil"? Consider having a movie night with your group and then discussing both individual and corporate evil as portrayed in the film. Take time to pray about the evil that is within and around you.

ON YOUR OWN:

This week, post the description of the armor of God (Eph. 6:10–20) in a place where you can meditate on it while you get dressed. Pray as you put on each corresponding piece of clothing that you would be able to stand firm against the spiritual forces of evil this week dressed in your "spiritual uniform."

NOTES

1. This section is based on *NIVAC: Daniel*, 174–188.
2. Longman, 178.
3. Longman, 181–182.
4. Longman, 183.
5. Longman, 187–188.
6. This section is based on *NIVAC: Daniel*, 188–198.
7. Longman, 190.
8. Longman, 196.
9. Longman, 198.

HOW LONG, LORD?

Daniel 8:1–27

Sometimes anticipation of change can be exciting, but at other times change appears impossible; patience seems pointless. The old-fashioned term for patience, "long-suffering," seems much more appropriate then, and trust becomes a tough action verb to live by. I can remember a canoe trip on a big lake against a fierce, unrelenting wind. I never thought I'd make it back to base camp and my family would have to somehow recover me at the bottom (or end) of the lake! Not even a hint of the kind of suffering that martyrs around the world face, even today, but still there was a moment when I cried out in my heart, "How long, Lord?" Daniel lived most of his life under the oppressive rule of foreign nations, and had a peek into the future of even more suffering to come for his people. Yet he was called on to trust in God's unfailing love and to teach that trust to others.

A RAM AND A GOAT[1]

Read Daniel 8:1–14.

1. From what we've learned from past visions, what do you expect the animals and horns to represent? How are they similar to previous visions? How are they different?

2. Think about verse 4: "I watched the ram as it charged toward the west and the north and the south. No animal could stand against it, and none could rescue from its power. It did as it pleased and became great." If you were in the midst of that situation, not knowing the outcome described in the next few verses, what might your feelings be? Can you think of modern-day equivalents? Personal equivalents?

3. Read Psalm 13. How might this psalm be helpful to a person living under the circumstances described in Daniel 8:4? How can it be helpful in your own circumstances?

4. How does the goat in 8:5–8 help you see the situation under the ram differently? How can it help you to prepare for whatever the next stage might be in your life?

5. From a human perspective, it might not be all that comforting to know that one ruler will topple the next if you still suffer under all of them. How is God's perspective different, as described in Psalm 2:1–6? Do you think the activity of Daniel 8:9–12 will merit a word of God's wrath?

6. What hope does 8:13–14 offer, even if the specifics are a bit hard to understand?

INTERPRETING THE VISION[2]

Read Daniel 8:15–27.

7. Compare Daniel's responses to his dream/vision in 7:15–16, 19–20 with the one in 8:15–16. What's different? How are the explanations different (compare 7:17, 23–25 with 8:19–25)?

[One] difference between the prophecies of the two chapters has to do with the nature of the animals and the transparency of the imagery.... We will see the ease with which we can associate these animals and their horns with particular and well-known political entities. This fact explains why commentators over the years have registered little of the interpretive disagreement that we saw in chapter 7.[3]

8. Keeping in mind that this vision takes place in the third year of King Belshazzar's reign (8:1), what impact would you expect it to have on Daniel? Looking back at Daniel 5 (which has to take place later than Daniel 8 since it was the last night of Belshazzar's reign), to what extent did Daniel use the information from his vision as an adviser in the king's court? Why might this be so (see 8:26)?

9. How far into the future does the vision extend (8:17, 19, 26)? What specifics do we know as a result of the interpretation (8:19–25)?

The ram with the two horns represents the "kings of Media and Persia" (v. 20). In the vision itself, one horn grew larger than the other, which is surely a reference to the fact that the Persian part of this empire soon swallowed the Median part and assumed dominance.

  The goat with the single horn that speedily devastated the ram is "Greece," the single horn being its first king—Alexander the Great.

He achieved an unprecedented domination from Italy to India in unbelievable time; but he died suddenly at age 33 in 323 BC, leaving behind two young sons, Alexander and Herakles. These boys were ultimately murdered, and the world was carved up between Alexander's [four] powerful generals, the Diadochi. The Diadochi are the "four prominent horns."[4]

10. Antiochus IV Epiphanes was a later ruler who descended from one of the Diadochi. The following passages from 1 Maccabees, one of the apocryphal books, describe what he did to Jerusalem:[5]

> *After subduing Egypt, Antiochus returned in the one hundred forty-third year. He went up against Israel and came to Jerusalem with a strong force. He arrogantly entered the sanctuary and took the golden altar, the lampstand for the light, and all its utensils. He took also the table for the bread of the Presence, the cups for drink offerings, the bowls, the golden censers, the curtain, the crowns, and the gold decoration on the front of the temple; he stripped it all off. He took the silver and the gold, and the costly vessels; he took also the hidden treasures that he found. Taking them all, he went into his own land. He shed much blood, and spoke with great arrogance. (1 Maccabees 1:20–24)*

> *And the king sent letters by messengers to Jerusalem and the towns of Judah; he directed them to follow customs strange to the land, to forbid burnt offerings and sacrifices and drink offerings in the sanctuary, to profane sabbaths and festivals, to defile the sanctuary and the priests, to build altars and sacred precincts and shrines for idols, to sacrifice swine and other unclean animals, and to leave their sons uncircumcised. They were to make themselves abominable by everything unclean and profane, so that they would forget the law and change all the ordinances. He added, "And whoever does not obey the command of the king shall die." (1 Maccabees 1:44–50)*

To what extent do these verses remind you of other kings Daniel has dealt with? To what extent does Antiochus seem worse?

Scholars almost universally agree that the horn that grew out of one of the four is the second century BC Seleucid ruler, Antiochus IV Epiphanes.... He started out small and grew large ... through the political manipulation for which he became famous (he was a "master of intrigue" [v. 23]), he managed to push his nephew out of the way and gain the throne....

Antiochus IV, however, established himself as a "completely wicked" and "stern-faced [fierce-looking] king" (v. 23) through his incredible intrusion and disruption of the Jewish ritual. Jewish religion and practice stood in the way of his policy of Hellenization....

Such actions against the formal worship of God's people was far more than an affront against the people; it was an attack against heaven itself. Antiochus indeed took a stand against the "Prince of princes," [8:25] that is, against God. But such arrogance can only lead to one conclusion: utter defeat.... [T]he ultimate power behind the Maccabean freedom fighters was God himself, who gave them the victory and allowed them to restore the temple to its former function as a center for worship of the true God.[6]

11. From Daniel's place in history, these events were still in the distant future (8:26). From our perspective, if the above interpretations are correct, they are documented history. How would Daniel's vision be an encouragement to the people living in Daniel's time? Does it still have any relevance for us? Explain.

12. Even with agreement by most scholars as to the interpretation of Daniel's vision, there is still confusion over how to interpret the specific number of 2,300 (8:14). What does this suggest to you about the interpretation of numbers in apocalyptic? What is the danger of reading too much into specific numbers (see Mark 13:29–36)? What can we learn from Daniel's conclusion in 8:27?

God calls us to live in the present while waiting with hope for the future.[7]

RESPONDING TO GOD'S WORD

IN YOUR GROUP:

Many times in the past, people have tried to interpret prophecies so specifically as to predict the specific day of Christ's return, in opposition to Mark 13:32: "But about that day or hour no one knows, not even the angels in heaven, nor the Son, but only the Father." Discuss what dangers such an interpretation can pose on believers' lives and attitudes.

ON YOUR OWN:

Think about situations in your own life that seemed utterly impossible to change. How have you seen God come through? Interview two or three other people about the same subject. Take time to praise God for the surprising ways he brings about change in impossible situations.

NOTES

1. This section is based on *NIVAC: Daniel*, 199–205.
2. This section is based on *NIVAC: Daniel*, 205–215.
3. Longman, 201.
4. Longman, 206.
5. New Revised Standard Version, 1994 edition.
6. Longman, 206–207.
7. Longman, 215.

HOW THEN SHOULD WE PRAY?

Daniel 9:1–27

Prayer is a discipline that is often under-practiced these days. We're all good at coming up with laundry lists of things we want from God, or even things our friends and family want, but you will find very few scriptural prayers that fit that model. Prayer can be much farther reaching, but is hard work, and often very humbling. Daniel takes a surprising turn in chapter nine, giving us a helpful model for prayer to think about, and an interesting peek into God's attitude toward prayer as well.

LEARNING FROM DANIEL'S APPROACH[1]

Read Daniel 9:1–4a.

1. Daniel 9:1 places this chapter during a time of historical transition—Darius, a Mede, takes over from the Babylonians. This is not a ho-hum change of leadership—it's the end of one world power replaced by a new world power. How does Daniel approach this time of uncertainty? What can we learn from his attitude?

2. Daniel understands from Jeremiah that the desolation of Jerusalem would last seventy years (9:2). Read Jeremiah 25:1 – 14 and 29:10 – 14 as possible Scriptures that Daniel might be referring to. How does the context of those Scriptures reveal what might be going on in Daniel's mind? What are the implications for God's people? For Nebuchadnezzar and the Babylonians? For God himself?

God uses human language to make his existence and nature known to us. In the Bible, he makes his will known to his people. Daniel understands this as he meditates on Jeremiah's letter.[2]

3. Historical records give pretty clear indicators that Nebuchadnezzar destroyed Jerusalem in 586 BC and Darius's first year of rule was 539 BC. How might the "seventy years" in Jeremiah provoke questions in Daniel's mind? What questions does it provoke in your mind?

DANIEL'S PRAYER[3]

Read Daniel 9:4 – 19.

4. List all the ways Daniel describes God. What is the overall impression you get of Daniel's God?

5. Now do the same thing for God's people. What do you make of the contrast between God and his people?

GOING DEEPER

At the heart of Daniel's prayer stands one of the most potent and pervasive theological themes of the Old Testament: the covenant.... It is a legal expression for a relationship where commitments are made and sanctioned by law, which have the force of penalties for noncompliance.... The legal relationship is best recognized as a political treaty. In other words, in the covenant/treaty God is the Great King, who enters into a political treaty with his servant people Israel.... The book of Deuteronomy follows the typical pattern of a treaty between the king of a powerful nation and the king of a relatively modest nation. This type of relationship is called a vassal treaty.[4]

6. What clues can you find from the wording in Daniel's prayer that show he is thinking about the "legal status" of God's people — where they stand in relation to God's law? From a legal perspective, how would you say God and his people have fared in their respective parts of the covenant?

7. Daniel consistently uses the pronoun "we" in his confession. From what you know of Daniel, would you include him in his own list of transgressions? Read your answer from question 5 using the pronoun "I" instead

of "God's people." Does it fit who you are? Now read Jeremiah 30:12–15. On what basis does Daniel look to God for help (9:18)?

8. From a human perspective, we might think God's people (and we our-selves) are a lost cause. However, God's plan takes into account the sort of people they are. Read Deuteronomy 30:1–10, God's addendum follow-ing the blessings and curses for obedience/disobedience. Do you think this plan would be regarded as "fair" in a courtroom? Is it consistent with God's character? How does Daniel build his prayer on this hope?

AN IMMEDIATE RESPONSE[5]

Read Daniel 9:20–27.

9. Gabriel's message might not add a lot of what we call "insight and under-standing" (9:22) in terms of specifics. But what does he teach Daniel about God's response to his prayer? What does Gabriel teach Daniel about his understanding of seventy years?

10. Do you get the sense that Daniel's prayer for the restoration of Jerusalem is answered? What will be involved in the process (9:24)?

11. Daniel relied on God's prophets and laws, and his own prayers, for guidance in a time of transition. Read Hebrews 1:1–4. How are our resources different today? How are they similar?

12. Consider the elements of Daniel's prayer that we've seen in this chapter: the way Daniel addresses God, his attitude toward himself and God's people, the laws he's broken, the judgment he's under, his petition to restore Jerusalem. For we who live under the new covenant established by Jesus (Matt. 26:26–30), what aspects of our prayers would be similar to Daniel's? What might be different?

GOING DEEPER

Jesus' death and resurrection is the foundation of our faith, not our repentance; but God calls us to repent of our sins to maintain a good relationship with him. As Paul states it, "[G]odly sorrow [over some infraction] brings repentance that leads to salvation" (2 Cor. 7:10). Daniel displayed this sorrow in the light of the sin of God's people, which moved him to repentance and restoration with God. Paul describes the same principle to the Corinthians and through them to us.[6]

RESPONDING TO GOD'S WORD

IN YOUR GROUP:

Think about the Lord's Prayer, as Jesus taught it in Matthew 6:9 – 13. What elements are similar to Daniel's prayer? What is different? Pray the Lord's Prayer together as a group.

ON YOUR OWN:

Have you ever fasted for a day? Not for dietary reasons, but simply as an act of humility and sincere petition to the Lord? If it is medically safe for you to fast for a specific period of time, consider choosing a day to do so, and to focus on praying for the establishment of God's kingdom, confessing on behalf of all Christians for the many ways we fall short of how God wants us to live.

NOTES

1. This section is based on *NIVAC: Daniel*, 216 – 223 and 228 – 229.
2. Longman, 228 – 229.
3. This section is based on *NIVAC: Daniel*, 223 – 225 and 229 – 234.
4. Longman, 230 – 231.
5. This section is based on *NIVAC: Daniel*, 225 – 228 and 234 – 243.
6. Longman, 240 – 241.

A GREAT WAR

Daniel 10:1 – 12:13

World War I was supposed to be the war to end all wars. Never before had so many countries come together to stomp out evil once and for all. Never before had war been known to take place in so many locations, use such advanced technology, take so many lives — it was a scale previously unheard of in history. And then World War II broke out. There is no end to wars in sight. Daniel gives us a glimpse into the wars of another time in history, and reminds us that as long as people live together in a sin-cursed world, war will be with us. But how does God view war? And how are we to understand all those wars in the Old Testament? Is there such a thing as a "great war" (Dan. 10:1)? Daniel gives us an unusual glimpse into what is happening behind the scenes in the wars that continue to plague us.

ON THE BANKS OF THE RIVER TIGRIS[1]

Read Daniel 10:1 – 11:1.

1. From a strictly human perspective, what do we know about Daniel and the people who were with him at the time of his

vision (10:2 – 8)? How does the heavenly being help us understand what Daniel was doing during his time of "mourning" (10:12, 14)?

2. Why did Daniel have to wait for three weeks to hear a response from God (10:12 – 14)? What does this tell you about the spiritual realm of things? Is it surprising to you? Explain.

3. What kinds of reactions do Daniel and the people with him have when the spiritual and physical world intersect (10:7 – 10, 15 – 19)? Do Daniel's reactions have any relation to God's view of him (see 10:11, 19)? Where else in Scripture do you see similar reactions (consider Gen. 15:1; 26:24; Judg. 6:23; Luke 1:13; Rev. 1:17)?

4. What does the role of "princes" seem to be as described in this chapter (10:13, 20 – 21)? What does it point to as one of the purposes of the agents of the spiritual realm (see Eph. 6:12 as well)?

We must be careful not to speculate on the hints the Bible gives us, but that there are spiritual powers, good and bad, behind the various human institutions is a truth taught in the Old Testament and ... in the New Testament as well.[2]

DANIEL'S FINAL VISION[3]

Read Daniel 11:2–45.

5. What is your overall impression of this vision? How does it compare to Daniel's other visions?

[This] vision ... is unlike any that have preceded it in Daniel. It begins with a lengthy prophecy about unnamed kings and their actions. While there is nothing similar to this prophecy in the Old Testament, we have examples from the broader ancient Near East.... This genre of prophecy, not using personal names, reads the details of history closely. Daniel 11 covers a period from the Persian period to the time of Antiochus Epiphanes. From what we know about the period we can affirm that the prophet writes with the accuracy of a historian. As a matter of fact, that is what many scholars feel is going on in this passage [this author not included]. That is, Daniel 11 is not a forward-looking prophecy from the standpoint of the sixth century BC, but rather a backward-looking history cast in the literary form of prophecy.[4]

6. What kind of message would this vision convey to Daniel about the future? About God? What glimpses do we have of the part God's people play during this time (11:14, 32–35)?

GOD IS A WARRIOR[5]

Read Daniel 12:1–13.

7. After all the complicated interactions and strivings of nations in Daniel 11, how is the final victory determined (12:1)? Who's the winner? What are the expectations for God's people (12:3, 7, 9–10, 13)?

GOING DEEPER

To more fully understand the cosmic war that lies behind this human conflict, we must situate the content of this chapter in the broader story of holy war in the Old Testament....

Holy war is a term never found in the Old Testament itself. However, the term is useful because it describes the character of warfare found there. At the center of holy war is Yahweh, the divine warrior. God fights on his people's behalf to give them the victory. Another way of stating the same truth is to say that God uses his people as a tool of his judgment against the evil of the world.... It is not that Israel does not fight, but they know that their victory is not a result of their own power and strategy, but because of God's fighting on their behalf.[6]

8. Conflict doesn't rest well with most of us. There's certainly plenty of people who throw up their hands at all the war in the Old Testament. There's been a lot of war since then done in the name of God that is far from godly. On an individual level, conflict tends to break down relationships, not bring them together, and it's certainly uncomfortable to deal with! But let's go to the source. What was the purpose of introducing conflict in Genesis 3:14–15?

9. Read Luke 1:68–79, Zechariah's prophecy following the birth of his son John the Baptist, as well as Colossians 2:15, speaking of Jesus' death on the cross. How does this language in the New Testament reflect the theme of holy warfare, as well as other imagery we've been looking at in Daniel? How does the conflict end?

10. John's vision in Revelation 1:9–20 has many similarities to Daniel's visions, but since it comes later in history, after the death of Jesus, it gives us a bit more detail. How do Jesus' words to John (Rev. 1:17–18) confirm his victory over evil? How did Jesus accomplish his victory?

GOING DEEPER

Daniel 10 indicates in a way rarely addressed in the Old Testament that there was already a cosmic-spiritual dimension to the warfare of old. Now we see that Satan has become the clear object of divine battle. The irony of the gospel is that that battle is won, not through killing, but rather by dying. Jesus, the warrior, accomplished his great victory by dying on the cross.[7]

11. Although victory over evil has been won through Jesus' death on the cross, we certainly still engage in plenty of conflict. We're in this "already–not yet" phase of history where the great war's end has been determined, but we're still engaged in skirmishes. Reread Ephesians 6:10–20 as well as Colossians 3:1–17 for clues as to how we're supposed to engage in the remaining spiritual battle. How are we called to imitate Christ during this last phase of the "great war"? Who or what is the enemy?

12. Tying this back into Daniel, what can God's people expect during the undefined length of time that remains until Jesus' final deliverance and return to his throne (12:7b, 10, 13)? How does God equip us to "go our way till the end" (Eph. 1:15–21)?

RESPONDING TO GOD'S WORD

IN YOUR GROUP:

One of the great hymns of the faith, which also portrays Jesus as the warrior in God's great war against evil, is Martin Luther's *A Mighty Fortress Is Our God*. Close your time together by singing this hymn and thanking God for his great victory in spite of the many struggles we may face in this world.

A MIGHTY FORTRESS IS OUR GOD[8]

A mighty fortress is our God, a bulwark never failing;
Our helper He, amid the flood of mortal ills prevailing:
For still our ancient foe doth seek to work us woe;
His craft and power are great, and, armed with cruel hate,
On earth is not his equal.

Did we in our own strength confide, our striving would be losing;
Were not the right Man on our side, the Man of God's own choosing:
Dost ask who that may be? Christ Jesus, it is He;
Lord Sabaoth,[9] His Name, from age to age the same,
And He must win the battle.

And though this world, with devils filled, should threaten to undo us,
We will not fear, for God hath willed His truth to triumph through us:
The Prince of Darkness grim, we tremble not for him;
His rage we can endure, for lo, his doom is sure,
One little word shall fell him.

That word above all earthly powers, no thanks to them, abideth;
The Spirit and the gifts are ours through Him who with us sideth:
Let goods and kindred go, this mortal life also;
The body they may kill: God's truth abideth still,
His kingdom is forever.

ON YOUR OWN:

As you conclude this study of Daniel, choose someone to partner with you, to pray for each other for ongoing wisdom, hope, and power as you "go your way to the end" (Dan. 12:13). Use prayers of Scripture such as Ephesians 1:15–21 or Ephesians 3:14–21 to guide you.

NOTES

1. This section is based on *NIVAC: Daniel*, 244–253.
2. Longman, 251.
3. This section is based on *NIVAC: Daniel*, 267–283.
4. Longman, 271.
5. This section is based on *NIVAC: Daniel*, 253–266 and 283–306.
6. Longman, 254.
7. Longman, 258.
8. Online March 2, 2009 at www.cyberhymnal.org/htm/m/i/mightyfo.htm
9. That is, "Lord of the armies of heaven."

LEADER'S NOTES

SESSION 1 LEADER'S NOTES

1. King Nebuchadnezzar besieged Jerusalem (1:1) and carried off some of the articles from the temple, placing them in his own god's temple (1:2). This was a common Near Eastern practice that demonstrated the dominance of one nation over another.[1] His training of the youths was a political tool for controlling Judah without actually taking over it. He placed Zedekiah, a puppet king, on the throne, and educated the youths in the ways and language of Babylon so that they could wield influence at a future time in Judah.

2. Daniel and his friends were well taken care of in the king's palace, and had great educational opportunities in Babylon — not a bad position to be in considering they were from a conquered nation. However, they were clearly under the control of the Babylonian king, facing compromises in their cultural and intellectual integrity. Dietary practices, worship regulations, freedom of thought, and their very identity in the changing of their names reflected the strong influence of Babylonian practices instead of their own Jewish culture.[2]

3. The Lord is given credit for the defeat of Jehoiakim, through Nebuchadnezzar, but for the purposes of the Lord nonetheless.

4. In addition to a kosher food regimen, Daniel's studies, particularly relating to omen or dream interpretation, do not fit with a Jewish mind-set. Nor can Daniel participate in any sacrificial or festival requirements. There are no restrictions against wine, unless a Nazirite vow has been taken. And the Babylonian names they've been given reflect Babylonian gods, taking away from their identity with the Jewish God. What is surprising is that Daniel chooses to make an issue of

food and wine, while not questioning other aspects of Babylonian culture that he is absorbing.

5. Bottom line, God's laws are intended to guide people toward what is best for them, which at the same time glorifies God for who he is. They are reminders of our need to depend on God, to trust him, and to be identified with him. They also demonstrate to the rest of the world how God protects and provides for his people. Even though Daniel was unable to observe all the Jewish laws in his circumstances, his voluntary dietary restrictions enabled him to remain distinct and remember his dependence on God on a daily basis. His trust in God was evident, reflecting the spirit of God's laws. But only the guard appointed over Daniel and his friends was aware of the food restrictions (1:11 – 16); it was not a public recognition of God's faithfulness to his people.

6. Only God could have made the young men look healthier on their more limited food regimen. God is clearly given credit for their growth in knowledge and understanding (1:17). Despite Nebuchadnezzar's control of the palace, God is clearly in charge of what is happening there.

7. God fills these chosen young men with such wisdom and knowledge that they surpass the wisdom of any others in the kingdom ten times over (1:20). As a result, God's young men are of great influence throughout the Babylonian kingdom, ironically doing what Nebuchadnezzar hoped to accomplish among Israelites by training the young men in Babylonian ways!

8. Joseph and Daniel were both young men when they were forcefully taken to another country. Yet they were both faithful, and God blessed them in all they did, giving them unprecedented opportunities of leadership in a foreign land. They both were given the ability to understand and interpret dreams, which were significant in their respective cultural contexts. In both stories, it is clear that God is sovereign over all nations, including Babylon, and uses circumstances that appear to be catastrophic to accomplish his own purposes. This was particularly good news to the Israelites in exile, who weren't sure if their God was still on their side, and if he would continue to act in favor of his people.

9. Living in a multicultural nation means that we are surrounded by different worldviews and practices that pressure and challenge us to live in ways other than what we may have been raised to believe. Some aspects of cul-

ture might be positive, negative, or neutral, but it is complex figuring out how to live in the midst of such an array of thought and action. With the advent of Christ, we have been given much greater freedom in understanding the laws and codes of conduct that are acceptable in God's kingdom. In fact, the expression of Christianity across different cultures can look quite different, though the central beliefs are the same. It is one of the great challenges of our day to differentiate what is truly Christian — what it looks like to live in God's kingdom — without confusing that with traditions that are simply part of a given culture.

10. Daniel accepts many of the changes that were forced on him without complaint — he had no choice over his name change (although he still referred to himself by his Hebrew name), or the kind of schedule he had to lead, or the education he would receive. However, he started with one thing — his diet — and went through the proper channels to try to hold onto a custom that would remind him of God and his power. When that failed, he privately went through another source, the guard, to persuasively do things his own way. Rather than reject his dreams and visions, he saw God working through them. He is a model of wisdom and discernment in the variety of ways he copes.

11. Answers will vary greatly on this question, depending on where you live, and what issues are more important to you. Some hot topics might include public policy on abortion and same-sex marriage, and personal ones such as living simply and with integrity in a world that usually does not. Strategies might vary as well, such as withdrawing from society, trying to change it, or engaging society in discussion while we live distinctly different lives.[3]

12. The New Testament is clear in its expectation of living in a hostile environment, just as Daniel lived in an environment that challenged his faith. We should be "shrewd as snakes, but innocent as doves," "living in it, but not of it," following faithful examples such as Paul to live a righteous life in the midst of an unrighteous world.

NOTES

1. Longman, 47.
2. Longman, 50.
3. For a more extensive discussion, see Longman, 62–69.

SESSION 2 LEADER'S NOTES

1. King Nebuchadnezzar requests not only an interpretation, but also for his wise men to tell him what the dream was. Some suggest he forgot the details of his dream, but most consider the king to be testing his wise men — it's much easier to come up with an interpretation that would please the king than to come up with the content of the dream on your own.[1] The wise men's repeated requests to hear the dream first (2:4, 7), and their response in 2:10 makes it clear that this is an unusual, and intimidating, request.

2. Daniel would agree that no wise man can discern the king's dream on his own (2:27). However, Daniel recognizes that all wisdom comes from God and, unlike the Babylonian wise men, knows that God's wisdom is accessible to those who seek it. He responds wisely, tactfully, to the king, but along with his friends turns to God for true wisdom through prayer.

3. Daniel and the king's advisers represent the greater contest between Daniel's God and the Babylonians' gods and between sources of wisdom. There are limits to what people can figure out on their own. Even in Daniel 1, it could be argued that Daniel was simply clever in the way he dealt with his circumstances — he could have used his own "smarts" to impress the king and get ahead. Daniel 2 leaves no doubt that the wisdom of God was necessary to pull Daniel and his friends out of a potentially life-threatening situation.

4. God is the giver of these dreams, as well as the giver of revelation when Daniel and his friends plead for his mercy. From Daniel's prayer of thanksgiving, God is the source of wisdom, knowledge, and power. He is sovereign over kings and mysteries. He knows about everything that is hidden to us and has the ability to make it known as he chooses.

5. Wisdom comes from God. Regardless of how far people go to obtain wisdom, they cannot get to the bottom of it — what we do learn in the way of wisdom comes from God and reflects his nature. Because the pursuit of wisdom is tied to God, wisdom is found in the context of relationship — it is more than a list of do's and don'ts, but rather an all-encompassing way to approach life.

6. In spite of present appearances, God is in control. It would seem that the all-powerful Nebuchadnezzar has his wise men over a barrel this time,

but God is the giver of dreams and the revealer of dreams—he is the one dictating the direction of the future, as well as the lives of his people. This is a great encouragement to the exiles, who live in circumstances out of their control. But it is particularly encouraging in light of the fact that God still chose to reveal his wisdom to a Jewish man, despite being outside the physical boundaries of Israel/Judah. As we face our own circumstances that seem out of control—either on a personal or national level—it is great comfort that God is in control, and that he lives in our midst, available to those who seek his wisdom.

7. Daniel and his friends not only live but are placed in high positions and receive many gifts from the king. The other wise men are spared as well. The king is awed by Daniel's God and prostrates himself before Daniel to show his honor. This is not to say that Nebuchadnezzar becomes a believer on the spot—but he is willing to add Daniel's God to his pantheon of gods as a worthy god to honor.[2] Although the interpretation of the dream points to Nebuchadnezzar's eventual demise, it also boosts the king's ego as the current king of kings, the gold head of the statue, in charge of all living things.

8. In 2:37, King Nebuchadnezzar is called the king of kings, yet he falls prostrate to Daniel who shows true wisdom as revealed to him by God. The passages in 1 Timothy and Revelation point to the true King of Kings, Jesus Christ, Son and heir of God at the end of all time and for eternity. Although King Nebuchadnezzar somewhat reflects God's glory by virtue of the fact that he is made a ruler by God over the known world at that time, he—like any human being—is nothing compared to the true King of Kings. Jesus' wisdom, power, goodness, and worthiness to receive worship as creator and redeemer of the world burst the boundaries of anything King Nebuchadnezzar could even imagine.

9. The progression of gold to silver to bronze to a mixture of iron and clay signifies growing weakness, unlike the notion that human culture gets better and stronger with time. Furthermore, the symbolism of a rock cut out, not by human hands, and ruling over all, points to the strength of God's kingdom over human kingdoms.

10. Jesus is frequently described as a rock, quoting from Psalm 118:22, "The stone the builders rejected has become the cornerstone." However, Jesus

did not establish a powerful kingdom on earth, but an everlasting kingdom over the entire universe with Jesus himself as the King of Kings ruling over everything. No one understood the scope of what he was doing until after his death and resurrection.

11. Christ *is* the power and wisdom of God (1 Cor. 1:24). The true wisdom of God is revealed completely to us in the person of Jesus. But it only makes sense to us when we submit our thoughts to God and believe his ways over ours. Putting our trust in Christ makes little sense from a philosopher's perspective, but it opens the door to the wisdom and power of God. The simple revelation of a dream completely outdoes Nebuchadnezzar, demonstrating the foolishness of God is wiser than human wisdom, and the weakness of God is stronger than human strength.

12. The full riches of wisdom and understanding are hidden in Christ (Col. 2:2 – 3). As we live united to Christ, we have the opportunity to grow in knowledge and wisdom, strengthened in faith and overflowing with thankfulness (Col. 2:6 – 7). Wisdom has more to do with putting off our old nature, receiving forgiveness for thinking we could do things our own way, and living in imitation of Christ — and less to do with deceptive philosophies or human traditions.

NOTES

1. Longman, 77 – 78.
2. Longman, 83.

SESSION 3 LEADER'S NOTES

1. (a) The long list of who is summoned (3:2, 3) brings to mind a large, influential crowd. The list isn't repeated in 3:7, but summarized as "all the nations and peoples of every language." This emphasizes the degree to which the kingdom is united in following Nebuchadnezzar's commands, and the difficulty for anyone to disobey.

   (b) The list of musical instruments used to summon worshipers (3:5, 7, 10, 15) adds to the pomp and circumstance of the occasion, and further emphasizes the control Nebuchadnezzar has over his empire—everything is done according to the specifications of the king.

   (c) Most often, but perhaps more subtle because it's such a long list, is the requirement at the heart of the passage (3:5, 7, 10, 12, 14, 15) that all people must serve Nebuchadnezzar's gods and worship the image of gold that he had made, or else be thrown into a fiery furnace (3:6, 11, 15). This might not be a big deal for the polytheistic Babylonians, but creates a huge problem for the Jews who are required to worship none but the true God.

2. King Nebuchadnezzar is extremely powerful, and feared by his subjects. He is prone to fury when he is crossed (1:10; 2:12; 3:13). He is quick to punish any disobedience with death (2:5; 3:6), but to reward with influential positions those who honor him (1:19; 2:6, 48; 3:15). You'd want to stay on his good side, or keep a healthy distance if you lived in his empire.

3. The people worship out of fear of the king and the consequences of disobedience. The astrologers seem a bit jealous of Shadrach, Meshach, and Abednego, and point out the Jews' lack of attention to the king to try to get a leg up, not out of jealousy for the king's reputation. The king is most enamored by himself and his unparalleled power.

4. "What god will be able to rescue you from my hand?" (3:15) lies at the heart of the issue. Who's stronger—God or Nebuchadnezzar? The Jews have a long history of God's rescues. From Abraham to Josiah, the last godly king of Judah, there's a strong record of God acting on behalf of his people, above and beyond the normal circumstances that human strength allows for. Who better to answer King Nebuchadnezzar's question than some Jewish youths?

5. Idolatry can be very subtle. Even the good gifts of God, when inordinately valued, can take the place that only God should have in our lives. The opinion of others, fear of looking good, a desire for control, a fear of confrontation, any number of things in creation (food, sex, money, education, recreation) — all of these can compete with the will of God in our lives.

6. Even though the youths were quiet about their faith, they were known as Jews and it made a difference. Though the heat (quite literally in this case!) can be uncomfortable, God uses these situations in our lives to make himself known to us and to test us — hopefully strengthening our faith as a result.

7. Shadrach, Meshach, and Abednego prove themselves to be courageous and faithful. Regardless of how God responds, whether he saves them from the furnace or not, they know his faithfulness and supremacy over Nebuchadnezzar, so they are not swayed by the king's threats. They worship God and God alone. Of course, living gives them a greater chance to prove the power and faithfulness of God to others, but their faith is not dependent on God's action — he has already shown himself to be true. We would do well to similarly trust God's purposes for us.

8. The details bring emphasis to the magnitude of the deliverance. For example, the furnace was so hot that there was no possibility of survival apart from God — as proven by the soldiers who died. Shadrach, Meshach, and Abednego's ties were immediately broken, allowing them to walk in the furnace, though the strongest soldiers bound them. The description of their clothing before and after points to the miraculous protection they had in the fire.

9. King Nebuchadnezzar himself recognizes the power of the God of Shadrach, Meshach, and Abednego. The Most High God (3:26) truly can rescue people from Nebuchadnezzar's own hand. As Nebuchadnezzar aligns himself with this God (at least for the time being), he promotes Shadrach, Meshach, and Abednego and calls for anyone opposing their God to "be cut into pieces and their houses be turned into piles of rubble" (3:29). Sadly, his professed worship of God has no effect on how he acts.

10. There is no question that the Most High God delivered them — the evidence was undisputed. Was this God himself, Jesus appearing in an early form? That question remains a mystery, but the result is the same: God

brought about a miraculous deliverance that proved his supreme power. All of Babylon heard of the great God of Shadrach, Meshach, and Abednego, and no one could say anything against him.

11. The text says nothing about the reaction or experience of Shadrach, Meshach, and Abednego, and yet it's hard to imagine them not being affected for the rest of their lives. Their faith was already strong, but this experience added a personal experience with God—an understanding of what it actually means for God to suffer alongside them and deliver them. Their suffering was also used by God to make his power clear to nonbelievers.

12. Today we typically don't see flashy miracles—such as saving people from a fiery furnace without even smelling of smoke. However, we live at a time when the revelation of God is complete—we've seen through Jesus what God is really like and, through Jesus' resurrection, the power of God. And that gives us great hope, because the power that raised Jesus from the dead is actually available to believers through Christ who lives in us. Not that our calling is to perform flashy miracles—we can leave that up to God when the time is right. But we are called to spread hope to others, the good news that God is with us, and that he gives us life when we were dead—he forgives us when there was no hope for life.

SESSION 4 LEADER'S NOTES

1. It seems a bit surprising to hear God's praise out of the mouth of this pagan king. Not only does he praise God in all humility, it is his pleasure to do so (4:2). Because these doxologies come directly from the king and are addressed to the nations and peoples of every language (4:1) — in fact, the very same people he addressed to bow down to his statue in chapter 3 — they have the feel of an official proclamation, wishing prosperity for all, and calling everyone in the known world to recognize the greatness of God.

2. Instead of a king who is full of himself and focused on his kingdom and his power, Nebuchadnezzar humbly acknowledges his position before God and God's eternal power and majesty. His furious anger (seen in earlier chapters) and his terror from his dream are replaced with the pleasure and peace of praising God.

3. The author could be emphasizing the wisdom of God that is only accessible by Daniel, far exceeding that of the other wise men. Alternatively, it is conceivable (though only a guess) that the wise men were afraid to give the king an interpretation because of its negative implications for the king. Even Daniel was terrified to tell Nebuchadnezzar his thoughts.

4. Nebuchadnezzar has been amazed at the wisdom of Daniel and his friends; he has marveled at Daniel's ability to recite his dream; his respect continues to grow when the Jewish friends survive his fiery punishment. But there's nothing like personal experience to make a lesson stick. King Nebuchadnezzar is transformed immediately from the most powerful person on earth to a creature no better than a beast for seven years. His transformation back to sanity happens just as quickly as it was lost. The extent of Nebuchadnezzar's praise seems to reflect a much greater humility and understanding of his place in the universe.

5. Repent or suffer the consequences! It seems so simple, and yet as human beings, we seem to learn better through suffering. Certainly it is better to trust God's ways and remain innocent than to sin and be restored. But God works through both means and develops our character in the process (see Rom. 5:3 – 5).

6. God protects his faithful people in spite of the odds. The earthly ruler who seems all-powerful is still subject to the even-more-powerful God. God's people have not been abandoned — justice can still prevail.

7. The deep waters that nourished the tree made it great (Ezek. 31:4–5, 7) because of God's plans for it to exceed all others in beauty (31:9). The tree's pride in its height (for no reason of its own) resulted in punishment — being cut down by other nations.

8. Both kings share a moment of pride looking over the kingdoms they have built during a time of peace. However, while God can truly look over his creation and take credit for all he made, Nebuchadnezzar's success is merely a gift from God, which was allowed for a brief time in history to accomplish God's purposes. It would be more appropriate for Nebuchadnezzar to give thanks to God than to take credit himself. Whereas God is king of heaven and earth for all eternity, Nebuchadnezzar is a man allowed to have rule over a small jurisdiction of God's earth for a short period of time.

9. Instead of trusting God's plan, accepting his limitations, and being content with his role in God's kingdom, Adam seeks to be more like God himself when he eats from the forbidden tree of knowledge (Gen. 3:6). As a result, God's entire kingdom is cursed, and humanity is sent outside the boundaries of the garden, God's dwelling place. Similarly, King Nebuchadnezzar has overreached his place and viewed himself in the position of God rather than a servant of God. He is forced to live outside the realm of his kingdom, living out his punishment among beasts.

10. Interestingly, both events take place in approximately the same area — Babylon was named for the tower of Babel. You could say that King Nebuchadnezzar has reunited the scattered nations of Babel under his united kingdom. A familiar pattern is beginning to emerge, where humankind is doing all it can to "reach to the sky," striving to become as powerful as God, and making a name for itself with no regard for God. In the case of Babel, God scatters the people and confuses one of the things that makes them uniquely human — their language. Similarly, God scatters Nebuchadnezzar to the edge of his own kingdom, and causes him to lose his reason, resembling a beast more than a human.

11. There is a tension between the psalmist's statement of belief in verse 1 and his envy of the arrogant and prosperous in subsequent verses — envy for people like King Nebuchadnezzar. At the root of his longings is the same desire as the wicked — to prosper and make a name for himself. He's

frustrated that faith in God the way he defines it—going to church, doing the right things—doesn't seem to get him ahead according to a worldly definition. His wants are actually dictated by earthly kingdoms rather than God's kingdom. His attitude results in a self-imposed separation from God that takes away from his humanity, just as God's judgment on King Nebuchadnezzar reduced him to a brute beast. The psalmist's struggle points to the struggle of every person—faithful or not—for either God's kingdom or something else.

12. The portrayal of Babylon as a tree being cut down is virtually identical to what we saw in Nebuchadnezzar's dream, and in Ezekiel. However, the stump imagery shifts from the restoration of Nebuchadnezzar's kingdom to the restoration of David's kingdom, which is eventually fulfilled by Jesus. Jesus, the only One who is truly glorious, the only One who is truly wise, who can rule with perfect justice, humbles himself in order to restore us to peace with God (see Phil. 2:6–11). Our only hope is in a God who reaches out to us in spite of our stubborn love of ourselves.

SESSION 5 LEADER'S NOTES

1. The same articles that were captured by Nebuchadnezzar in chapter 1 are being used in Belshazzar's banquet. The seemingly all-powerful king is terrified by a sign from God. The king calls for his wise men, promising great things to anyone who can interpret the sign, but they are unable to help him. Daniel is the only one in the kingdom with access to wisdom from God for the answer.

2. The introduction of two new characters jumps out the most — King Belshazzar and the queen. In addition, the human hand is a strange, new sign, unheard of before now. Clearly, some time has passed, and the relationship between Daniel and the king seems more distant, even strained.

3. Nebuchadnezzar and Belshazzar seem to have pretty similar ruling styles — a great show of power and pomp; willingness to grant great gifts to those who help them; reliance on enchanters, astrologers, and diviners for wisdom; belief in numerous gods; but great fear at a true sign from God. Belshazzar seems more daring and disrespectful against the God of Jerusalem, and a bit more dubious of Daniel as a wise man.

4. Daniel's tone and the content of his speech indicate that he is not at all impressed by Belshazzar. He begins by refusing the king's offer of gifts. He gives Belshazzar a stinging rebuke — he spoke to Nebuchadnezzar much more gently and respectfully, despite his pride. Nevertheless, Daniel is committed to delivering God's message to him accurately. In this case, God's judgment on Belshazzar matches Daniel's own mood. But the message is still delivered with restraint by Daniel, and the king does reward him for his interpretation. Our own reactions can often reflect our own desires rather than God's, and include a whole lot more emotion when provoked. It takes great wisdom to respond to provocation in a godly way!

5. Job understands God's control over life and death, and his rightful position of determining what will be in the lives of his creation. Belshazzar, by contrast, attributes power to the creation, not the creator, when he praises the gods of silver and gold, of bronze, iron, wood, and stone (5:4, 23). But his true allegiance is to himself, daring God through his actions to stop him from his arrogant and blasphemous claims. Think carefully about the discussion in session 3 regarding idols (question 5) before you answer which position reflects the worldview that you *live*.

6. In chapter 4, Daniel's Babylonian name is used six times, either directly by the king, or stated parenthetically by the narrator, whereas Daniel is mentioned only twice. In chapter 5, Belteshazzar is used only once, in reference to King Nebuchadnezzar, and the remaining six times, Daniel is used. It could be argued that the closeness of names (Belteshazzar and Belshazzar) would be too confusing to use together in chapter 5. However, the names also reflect the fact that Daniel helped to *protect* Nebuchadnezzar's [*the king's*] *life* and restore him to his kingdom through Daniel's numerous introductions of Nebuchadnezzar to the Most High God's wisdom and power. Belshazzar, on the other hand, received only *God's judgment* through Daniel because of his unrelenting pride. We worship a God who both protects us and judges us, reflecting his love and mercy, as well as his justice. The two would seem at odds with each other if it weren't for God's unique solution of taking the punishment of us all on himself, through Jesus, so that he could protect us from his just wrath.

7. At one level, we can never know the mind of God. How he determines a person's final judgment is not for us to know, and we are grateful for the patience of God to defer his judgment for a little while longer. But we do know that God knows the inclinations of our hearts. And he does hold us responsible for what we do know. Belshazzar, knowing the history of Nebuchadnezzar (5:22), was aware of what the Most High God could do, yet he set himself up against this God anyway. Using the goblets from the temple in Jerusalem was like spitting in God's face, and he pays for his blasphemy the same night.

8. "I know I'm not perfect" is a common enough phrase that expresses most people's recognition that they don't meet the mark when it comes to God's standards. How you feel about that is likely to vary with your understanding of Christ's role in your life (see next question).

9. God's justice is regarded with joy. He himself works salvation for the righteous, but terror for evildoers. When it's all said and done, there's nothing in between. God himself makes this possible. No one but Jesus could ever satisfy God's standards, but all the punishment his children deserve is taken on by his own Son, Jesus, so no one else, in heaven or earth, can bring any charge against any of God's own. All sin — past, present, and

future—has already been accounted for by Jesus. This is the great news of the gospel!

10. When Jesus came, he established greater freedom from ceremonial law. We are "off the hook" in some respects. But at the same time, he clarified the moral law in a way that cuts much deeper and makes it clear that no one can keep God's standards. Grace doesn't exist so that we have the freedom to sin all the more, but rather to equip us to live joyfully in a way that pleases God (Rom. 6:1–7). Setting ourselves up against the Lord of heaven has more to do with an attitude toward God than specific acts, though the acts point back to the state of our hearts. Pride is probably the biggest factor that indicates our attitude against God and against our neighbor, as we abuse the privileges he's given us to live our lives on this earth.

11. As God's prophet, Daniel was acting very specifically as the voice of God against Belshazzar. We are not in the same position. Only God can judge. We condemn ourselves by any judgment we make, since we ourselves break any standard we use against others. While much can be gained by speaking the truth in love to those we are in a relationship with, we should do so with great sadness about any sin and with great hope for restoration to God's ways. We would do well to examine ourselves first and remove the logs out of our own eyes so that we approach any sinner with humility as fellow sinners.

SESSION 6 LEADER'S NOTES

1. "We have seen the Hebrew sage climb the political ladder from captive prisoner to initiate to sage (ch. 1) to chief sage (ch. 2) to administrator over the province of Babylon (chs. 2–3) to the king's personal adviser (ch. 4) to third ruler in the kingdom (ch. 5) to the prime minister that the king himself intends, at the beginning of ch. 6, to set over the entire kingdom and does implicitly set over the kingdom at the end of ch. 6."[1] This political climb tells us something of Daniel's wisdom, but even more of God's providence and protection of his man in Babylon. In spite of present appearances, God is in control. The theme is consistent throughout Daniel, and a great encouragement to the exiles of Daniel's day—Daniel not only survives, he prospers.

2. Daniel 6 is most similar to Daniel 3. In both chapters, a jealous group of administrators go to the king to make trouble for Jews on the grounds of their faithful worship. The Jews are punished by the king, but an angel protects them and the king punishes the jealous administrators in their place. The king commands everyone to worship the Most High God (in addition to the Babylonian gods). The story line is basically the same, though the characters and punishments are different. However, Daniel takes it one step further than his friends. Not only does Daniel not bow down to something other than God, he continues to pray to his own God and seek help. The attitudes of the kings are quite different as well. Whereas Nebuchadnezzar is furious at the response of Shadrach, Meshach, and Abednego, Darius is dismayed that he's unwittingly caused trouble for Daniel and does everything he can to try to save him, not resting until he learns of Daniel's great rescue by God.

3. I think we'd be disappointed by now if we didn't see Daniel continue to distinguish himself and live up to such high standards. The passage in 1 Peter almost seems written with Daniel in mind—written to people with an exile mentality, challenged to live so uprightly that people accusing them end up glorifying God. Peter's standard seems pretty hard to attain—in chapter 1 he actually challenges people to live holy lives because God himself is holy (1 Peter 1:15–16). Daniel puts more flesh on the description—an example of someone who did live this way! But it still

seems an impossible standard to achieve without God himself giving us the ability.

4. The administrators and satraps are trying to manipulate King Darius, at the expense of Daniel, as well as testing Daniel in his faith. Though the king is led along by their plot, the schemers (and their families) are the ones who fall into their own trap. Daniel prospers, and God's name is praised throughout the kingdom.

5. The law traps the king himself—the person who created it—into something he has no desire to do, but cannot change because of the nature of the law code. God's justice occurs, even though the king's hands are tied by the law. Daniel is saved and the unrighteous administrators are destroyed. That doesn't always happen on this earth, but ultimately, we are assured that God's justice prevails (Ps. 73:18–19). Regardless of the state of weak human laws, we can have hope in God's justice. Furthermore, the king's first edict for all to worship him alone for thirty days is superseded by his later decree that people in every part of his kingdom must fear and reverence the God of Daniel (Dan. 6:26).

6. God's law, as described in Psalm 19, is refreshing, trustworthy, right, radiant, pure, sure, precious, sweet, giving joy, and enduring forever. Everything about it is life-giving, whereas the law given by Darius, in this example, is one that would cause only fear and punishment, not to mention a faulty judgment.

7. The two statements about God's law have to be consistent, or neither would be true. So logically speaking, if we truly love God and neighbor as he intended, we will experience refreshment of our souls and joy in our hearts. The problem occurs when we are more convinced of our own "laws" than God's—we seem determined to love ourselves and the things God created more than God and neighbor, and we suffer the consequences.

8. The king's law has no effect on Daniel whatsoever. As 6:10 states, "When Daniel learned that the decree had been published, he went home to his upstairs room where the windows opened toward Jerusalem. Three times a day he got down on his knees and prayed, giving thanks to his God, just as he had done before." He did not publicly speak out against the king, but quietly continued praying to God as he had always done. In the short run,

he had to endure a night with lions, but in the long run, his obedience to God was honored and Daniel prospered.

9. Like Daniel, Joseph prospered in all that he did and progressed from the status of a slave to the second highest in command in all Egypt. Joseph was faithful to God, but even more than that, God was faithful to his people, and put Joseph in a position where he could influence the greatest ruler of the day, and protect and provide for his people. Even when people intended evil for Joseph, God used it for good.

10. Perhaps the apostles were thinking of Daniel when they proclaimed to the Sanhedrin that they must obey God rather than human beings (Acts 5:29). They recognized that their obedience to God would be compromised if they listened to the high priests, who were filled with jealousy, just like the administrators in Daniel's time. God's angel freed the apostles, just as he protected Daniel from the lions, enabling them to continue on with God's work. God overcomes the evil intents of people in order to accomplish his purposes — the salvation of his people and proclamation of his name.

11. It's hard not to picture Jesus' tomb when the stone is rolled in front of the mouth of the lions' den and sealed. Like Daniel, Jesus was arrested while praying, also under false pretexts. At the light of dawn, both are found alive. However, unlike Daniel who had the protection of an angel, Jesus died a horrible death. He went through with his undeserved punishment for the sake of reconciling God to all of humankind, taking God's justice onto himself. If Jesus' time on the cross was an ordeal like Daniel's, testing his innocence before God, his death would suggest his guilt — and indeed Jesus had our guilt upon him — but his resurrection proved his innocence.

12. Take some time on your own to think about this question. First, pray for wisdom to discern where God's law may be compromised. Pray for strength to remain faithful. Pray for others who may face similar or even more challenging circumstances. Praise God for his faithfulness.

NOTE

1. D. N. Fewell, *Circle of Sovereignty: A Story of Stories in Daniel 1–6,* Journal for the Study of the Old Testament Supplement 72 (Sheffield, England: JSOT, 1988), 154, quoted in Longman, 164.

SESSION 7 LEADER'S NOTES

1. There's not much context for this chapter, other than the fact that it is at the beginning of Belshazzar's rule—it's just a description of Daniel's dream, and the images are not very familiar. Churning seas, strange beasts, emerging horns, and terms we're not accustomed to in everyday language ("Ancient of Days", "son of man") make for a confusing plot line. There seems to be an order to it, but it's hard for our rationally oriented minds to make much sense of it. In a nutshell, a series of beasts that are quite violent are destroyed by this Ancient of Days who will win in the end.

2. Just from 7:2–3, the "great sea" seems like a dangerous place—winds churning up waves, and beasts coming out of it. The other verses support that impression—that God holds it back in order to contain its damage, and ultimately in the sinless world of the new heavens and earth, the sea and its evil will be gone.

3. The beasts are all something out of a nightmare. The animals portrayed—lion, eagle, bear, and leopard—are all beasts of prey and seem quite eager to devour flesh. Multiple heads and iron teeth go beyond reality, serving only to magnify the fright. There doesn't seem to be any place to escape to. In each case, the beasts seem to be ruling over and crushing humanity, and are against God's purposes.

4. The beasts, except for the bear, are creatures that do not exist in God's creation. God created both plants and animals "according to their kinds," whereas the beasts of Daniel 7 are combining features of distinct kinds of animals. Deuteronomy 22 shows further concern for keeping things separate. The beasts are a violation and perversion of God's creation. Furthermore, the beasts are ruling over humankind rather than vice versa.

5. Thrones represent authority and judgment. White clothing represents purity or righteousness, and white hair indicates old age and wisdom. Fire often represents judgment. Thousands of attendants mean a large kingdom. An open book suggests a court case that's still in progress. A body destroyed and thrown into a blazing fire demonstrates complete destruction. Clouds of heaven tend to conjure God and heaven. "All nations and peoples of every language" suggests the whole world. God is clearly the victor and will reign eternally.

6. Man is made in the image of God, so it is appropriate to see God, the Ancient of Days, pictured in Daniel as a man or son of man. Cloud and fire imagery is often associated with God—in the wilderness leading the Israelites, on top of Mount Sinai, and riding the clouds in various psalms. The story of the Old Testament is how God is in control and victorious over any foe, and that message clearly comes through in Daniel 7 as well—a message of great comfort, particularly following some very nasty beasts.

7. Like Daniel, we would love to have more clarification! He turns to an angelic being to help interpret the dream, but initially only gets a summary in the broadest terms (7:17). When Daniel presses him for more specifics, his interpreter gives a little more detail, but nothing that helps to define specific kings or the timing of events that would satisfy our curiosity. Our interpretations should not go beyond what God has revealed.

8. As long as you are in the category of holy people belonging to the Most High, there is a promise of ultimate victory and everlasting life in his kingdom (7:27). Great news if you are the underdog in a powerful earthly kingdom! However, it is rather disturbing to consider how many long, cruel kingdoms will arise, viciously oppressing God's people. It's not something that we can expect relief from anytime soon.

9. Paul's conclusion is that we all act like beasts—none of us is righteous. Our words and actions are quick to hurt others in whatever "kingdom" we have authority in, as we participate in the struggle *against* God rather than *with* him against evil.

10. "Individual sinners are harmful, sometimes deeply. But sinners bound together behind a group cause can cause great devastation. Nationalism, racism, sexism, denominationalism, factionalism—great evil can arise when sinners come together with a common purpose against someone outside of the group, the 'other.' We can depersonalize the other; they aren't quite human, and so to harm the other is not quite the same as hurting one of our own."[1]

11. Paul helps us to see the spiritual forces of evil that are behind the earthly forces of evil. We are not fighting other people, but evil itself—which is in us as much as it is in other people. The spiritual armor that we are to wear reflects Jesus himself, as we "put on" his righteousness, peace, and

salvation. We are to pray at all times, availing ourselves of the power of God himself to fight evil—whose power, we see in Daniel 7, cannot be matched by the evil forces.

12. Revelation 13 uses the same imagery as Daniel 7 to describe the beast who boastfully battles against God, luring the people of the world to worship him, and making war against God's people. Daniel, Paul, and John all consistently exhort God's people to patiently wait with endurance and faith for the promised victory that God will, without a doubt, accomplish. John tells us that Jesus is the son of man coming with the clouds, and it is he who "loves us and has freed us from our sins by his blood, and has made us to be a kingdom and priests to serve his God and Father" (Rev. 1:5–6). It is because of Jesus, and Jesus alone, that we have the sure hope that we will be among the faithful.

NOTE

1. Longman, 197.

SESSION 8 LEADER'S NOTES

1. There's a certain expectation that animals represent nations or rulers, and they exert a lot of power over people. As in Daniel 7, there's a sequence of rulers, and each seems more powerful than the next. God's people seem to suffer under these rulers, but they always seem to point to an end where God reverses things. These animals are not quite as fearful as in Daniel 7 — they're not beasts of prey, nor are they combining different animal features, except that they have unusual horns. But they do seem more bent against God and his heavenly host.

2. It seems like a hopeless situation — a powerful ruler who can't be stopped. You might feel the frustration of standing by watching without knowing what to do, or fear for your life and loved ones if you happen to live under the rule of such a figure. Modern-day equivalents might be nations with harsh dictators, countries where genocide is taking place, or where the ruler takes advantage of all the countries' resources without taking into consideration the concerns of the people. At a more personal/individual level, there are many situations where you feel powerless and circumstances seem impossible to change.

3. Although the psalm was written of David in his particular circumstances, it gives voice to the feelings of any desperate situation such as in 8:4, or difficult circumstances any of us may be facing. It helps the person reciting it to put feelings into words, and addresses the complaint directly to God, rather than just mulling over the problems. The psalm concludes with a statement of faith and trust — a reminder that God is good and is sovereign over both our circumstances and our enemies.

4. The ram is not invincible after all. Over time, other rulers more powerful come and go themselves. Although the goat was so powerful, it also was replaced by other more powerful rulers (horns). There's a sense in which we should be prepared for difficult rulers and/or circumstances over the long haul. Our hopes should not be geared toward "getting through" any particular stage, but rather enduring and relying on other resources for our strength.

5. God is sovereign over all the nations. He might let them exert their power for a while, but he laughs and scoffs at them. In a moment, God can change the circumstances and raise up rulers whenever he chooses. But his

chosen King rules over all. The situation in 8:9–12 seems quite specifically against God and his people, which might merit his action—although the wording in 8:12 suggests that it might be because of the rebellion of God's own people that all this is happening in the first place, in which case he might wait a little longer.

6. The "holy ones" are in conversation about the problem at hand, and there is a number of days given as to when the sanctuary will be reconsecrated. In spite of the apparent chaos, God is still in control.

7. In Daniel 7, Daniel takes initiative to get an explanation from one of the holy beings, but doesn't get much more information than he originally dreamed. In Daniel 8, a voice—presumably the very voice of God—tells Gabriel to give Daniel an explanation, and it is much more specific.

8. Daniel's dream in chapter 8 puts a lot of specific future information in the hands of someone living during the Babylonian empire! It could be very humbling in the hands of someone like Daniel, or perhaps cause fear regarding who the next ruler will be and how he will come to power. In the hands of someone less godly, you could imagine it being used to advance his own power. There's no indication that Daniel made known any of his knowledge to the Babylonian king or wise men, nor did he allow it to color his interpretation of the writing on the wall. Daniel is told by Gabriel to seal up the vision in 8:26, and he seems to have done so obediently.

9. Daniel is told the vision concerns the time of the end, the time of wrath, the distant future. From our perspective, that usually means the end of time as we know it, but from Daniel's perspective, it apparently points ahead to the second century BC, because it was fulfilled then, at least in part. Daniel is specifically told about Media, Persia, and Greece, and told with less detail about another wicked king, a master of intrigue, who will eventually be destroyed also.

10. The removal of holy vessels is reminiscent of King Nebuchadnezzar as mentioned in Daniel 1. King Belshazzar was worse than Nebuchadnezzar when he profaned the holy vessels in Daniel 5. They were returned when the exiles returned to Jerusalem and rebuilt their temple during the time of the Persians. However, the commands of the Greek king Antiochus take things to another level. Instead of profaning the holy vessels himself, he

orders the Jews themselves to do so, and much worse, as he forces them to build their own pagan altars and defile themselves in many ways.

11. Consistent with the theme of Daniel, this vision shows how God is in control in spite of the circumstances people faced. Although the people of Daniel's time wouldn't have understood all the specifics, they were reminded that God could change what seemed impossible to change. The fact that Daniel's vision is consistent with the historical record should be all the more encouraging to us. God is true to his word and has the power to make what he says really happen. Furthermore, our understanding of Daniel 8 should help us to trust the other promises of God that have not yet been fulfilled, even if we don't understand all the specifics. Faith is believing what is unseen (Heb. 11:1), and God has not changed; we can continue to trust him for our future just as Daniel trusted him many centuries ago.

12. We should be leery of trying to figure out numbers too closely in apocalyptic. "[I]f we cannot be certain of numbers used in prophecies that have already been fulfilled, how likely can we figure out the numbers that point to times in the far distant future?"[1] Jesus was very clear about the impossibility of predicting the end of time. Like Daniel, it's okay for us to admit some things are "beyond understanding" (8:27). Our job is to be ready when the time comes, not to know when that time is.

NOTE

1. Longman, 208.

SESSION 9 LEADER'S NOTES

1. Daniel is studying the Scriptures for guidance as to how to approach this time of change. He turns to Jeremiah as God's spokesperson to gain understanding, and to God himself in prayer for further petition. Daniel's prayer is earnest and is characterized by a humble attitude of fasting, petition, and confession. God's Word is not always the first place we turn to for wisdom in the context of political turmoil. Nor do we always start with an attitude of confession. But Daniel gives us a glimpse into how a godly leader approaches the resources God has made available to us for guidance and wisdom.

2. Jeremiah makes it very clear that God's people brought on the exile through their own disobedience to God's covenant. Nebuchadnezzar was a tool in God's hand to punish his people for not listening to him. Now that Nebuchadnezzar is gone, Daniel might understand this time to be a time of change, the time when God will restore his people, if they seek him with all their hearts (Jer. 29:13). His prayer demonstrates action consistent with his thoughts: it is time for humility and repentance. The implications for God's people are clear — God holds them accountable for their actions, but there is also hope for the future if they repent and have a better attitude toward God. Nebuchadnezzar and the Babylonians have now been shown to be vulnerable like any other nation — simply tools of God, not the all-powerful kingdom they thought themselves as. God shows himself to be true to his word — he is the true sovereign ruler dictating the rise and fall of nations. What he says will be accomplished, which adds weight to his words of hope for the future.

3. Remember that the years before Christ (BC) are numbered from 1 BC backward, so that 586 BC was *earlier* than 539 BC. If you do the math, forty-seven years have passed. The Babylonians are now gone. Daniel might understand the seventy years symbolically, representing a generation, in which case it might mean he's wondering if the time of exile is over. Or he might understand it literally, in which case he might be wondering if Jerusalem will be restored within the next twenty-three years, and contemplating how he might be influential in helping that come to pass. We probably have similar questions, but also more general questions as to

how literally we should understand such numbers, and how this situation helps us understand similar statements in other parts of Scripture.

4. God is great and awesome, and keeps his covenant of love (9:4). He sent servants to speak to the kings and people of the land (9:6). God is righteous (9:7, 14). God is merciful and forgiving, even in the face of rebellion (9:9). God is true to his word, even when it is against his people (9:12). God brought his people out of Egypt with a mighty hand and made a name for himself (9:15). Overall, Daniel gives a picture of a consistently fair yet merciful and patient God, who never changes, and loves his people.

5. God's people have sinned and done wrong; they have been wicked and rebelled; they have turned away from God's commands and laws (9:5, 9–11). They have not listened to warnings (9:6). All God's people are covered with shame because of their sin (9:7–8). They have not changed their ways in response to disaster (9:13). They do not obey God (9:14–15). They have given God a bad name (9:16). God's people could not be more of a contrast to God. Their only consistency is in their disobedience. They continually go against their God who has been so merciful to them.

6. Daniel's language in 9:4 specifically refers to the covenant, then continually refers to the keeping or breaking of commands and laws (9:5, 10, 11), particularly mentioning kings as well as common people (9:6, 8, 11). Daniel refers to the fulfillment of the law of Moses in regard to the curses and judgments that have occurred (9:11), a more specific reference to the covenant law. God consistently keeps his side of the law, including the curses for disobedience, while his people continually break their side of the law.

7. From a human perspective, Daniel seems like a righteous man. In fact, we saw in 6:4–5 that his coworkers knew they wouldn't be able to find a charge against him unless it involved his allegiance to his God. And yet he identifies with the corporate sin of his people—we are all rebellious against God in our hearts and actions. None of us is righteous (Rom. 3:10). There is no hope for us if God's mercy has anything to do with our own actions or attitudes. But Daniel appeals to God based on God's reputation and his great mercy, not Daniel's or anyone's righteousness.

8. God's plan is not fair—it is merciful. Although he carries out justice through his curses, his purposes go beyond that—his desire is to restore

his people to a place where he can bless and protect them, while they are obedient to him. Only then will his people be truly happy, and his name be glorified. Daniel appeals to this promise of God, seeking him with all his heart, so that he and his people might be restored in their relationship with God, their only hope.

9. "As soon as you began to pray, a word went out" (9:23). God clearly hears our prayers and has an immediate answer. Most of us will not have the opportunity to peek behind the curtain, as it were, to have a messenger tell us about the inner workings of God's answers. But Gabriel's message allows us to see that when God responds to our prayers, we don't necessarily see the answers in a way we would understand them. In fact, Gabriel's explanation doesn't add a whole lot to our understanding—except perhaps to clarify that understanding seventy years simply as seventy years is a bit too simplistic. God has things under control, but it's not for us to know the details.

10. However you interpret seventy "sevens," there is a point at which transgression, sin, and atonement will be completed. And everlasting righteousness and anointment of the holy will occur. It sounds like things will be rough for awhile, but eventually God will be victorious.

11. Jesus offers the clearest understanding of God that we can have. Daniel didn't have revelation that was as complete, but we do. Nor did Daniel have the purification for sins that Jesus provides at the time that he lived. We do. But our understanding of Jesus still comes through God's word, which is now complete in the Old and New Testaments. We still need to look to God's Word, and seek out his wisdom through prayer, just as Daniel did.

12. God has not changed, nor have our sinful hearts. So our praise of God would remain the same, as would the need for us to repent on a regular basis of our sinful attitudes. Jesus made it even clearer than Mosaic law that we are incapable of keeping the intent of God's law (see for example the Sermon on the Mount in Matt. 5–7). However, we can also thank God for the punishment that Jesus has taken for us—we are no longer subject to exile or any of the other curses. The Anointed One that he promised has come so that we might be fully restored to God. At the same time, the restoration has not been accomplished in full—Jesus is not yet

reigning fully on earth. So instead of praying for the restoration of Jerusalem, it would be appropriate for us to pray for the establishment of Jesus' kingdom on earth, for God's patience as others come into the kingdom, but also that Jesus would come quickly to put a final end to sin and its consequences.

SESSION 10 LEADER'S NOTES

1. Daniel was in mourning for three weeks. During that time he had a restricted diet and didn't use any lotions. When he was standing on the river bank of the Tigris, he saw a vision but none of the people with him did — they were just overwhelmed with terror and hid themselves. The heavenly being makes it clear that Daniel was humbling himself before God as he tried to gain understanding regarding the future of his people.

2. Daniel was heard immediately, but the heavenly messenger was held up for three weeks by the prince of the Persian kingdom until Michael came to help him out. It's hard to imagine an earthly prince holding up one of God's angels, so this is presumably an angel on the "dark" side. This tells us that there's spiritual activity going on that we're normally unaware of. Good and bad forces are battling each other that we can't see or hear, or even sense most of the time. Because it's beyond our usual capacity to perceive, it can be surprising to get a peek into this other world.

3. Daniel's companions were terrified and fled. Daniel himself seems to faint dead away. Even after he's revived he's trembling and speechless until the heavenly being strengthens him — he can hardly breathe! Daniel is told twice that he's highly esteemed by God and shouldn't be afraid — it's just a bit much for a mere human! Just about any time the heavenly realms intersect with the physical world, God's representative has to assure his hearers that there's nothing to be afraid of — examples include Abraham, Isaac, Gideon, Zechariah, and John, but this is not an exhaustive list.

4. The princes are part of spiritual armies that fight against each other in the battle between good and evil. Michael and the heavenly being speaking to Daniel are mentioned on God's side; the princes of Persia and Greece are on the other side. They seem to be fighting wars in the spiritual realm at the same time that struggles are going on in the physical world.

5. This vision is much longer and more detailed than Daniel's other visions. It almost reads like a military planning book or historical account.

6. The great detail underscores God's knowledge and control of the future, which would be a message of hope for Daniel and his people. There are a lot of political struggles and wars, as well as struggles for God's people, but ultimate victory is in God's hands. God's people seem pretty power-less overall. In 11:14, those who are violent rebel, but without success. In

11:32–35, those who are wise are involved in instruction, but also persecution, being refined by God in the process.

7. The battles among nations seem endless until Michael steps in. When he does, God's people are delivered. The victory is clear—God has been in control all along. God's people don't suddenly become powerful in their own right—in fact, 12:7 suggests a brokenness of God's people before the end is accomplished. Overall, the message to Daniel seems to be to wait (12:9, 13), and to expect to be refined in the process (12:10), while leading others in the ways of wisdom and righteousness (12:3).

8. God's curse on the serpent meant that there would be a separation between the serpent and Adam and Eve. Enmity would keep them apart both physically and mentally—who really wants to hang around with snakes? God made it easier for Adam and Eve (and us) to stay away from the source of evil by making it reprehensible. But by introducing this conflict, God was also pointing ahead to using the offspring of Adam and Eve to crush the serpent—good conquers evil. Without such conflict, we would be lured all the more into the ways of evil.

9. Zechariah's prophecy at the birth of Jesus announces the culmination of all that we've been talking about in Daniel—in spite of all that has happened through history, God is in control, bringing victory on behalf of his people. The image of the horn of salvation (Luke 1:69) contrasts to the many horns we've seen in Daniel's other visions (Dan. 7–8). The warrior language comes through clearly in Luke 1:71, 74—rescue from our enemies. God's mercy following the fulfillment of covenant curses comes through in Luke 1:72–75. And God's call to his people to turn many to righteousness (12:3) continues with John the Baptist's role (Luke 1:76–77). In Colossians 2:15, Jesus' death on the cross, which seals the victory against the conflict with evil, is put into military terms—God the warrior is the victor.

10. Jesus tells John that he holds the keys of death and Hades (Rev. 1:18). He is in charge now. But he accomplished it through his death, not through the means of battle that we are accustomed to.

11. According to Ephesians 6, we are called to be warriors, imitating Christ as we put on our spiritual armor. But our enemy is the spiritual forces of evil (Eph. 6:12), and we fight the flaming arrows of the evil one (Eph. 6:16) as

we persevere with truth, righteousness, peace, and salvation. Colossians 3 gives us further insight into how we fight the "great war." We are to die to ourselves as Christ did, putting to death whatever belongs to our earthly nature (Col. 3:5–11), and "putting on" the new self that follows after the image of God (Col. 3:10–17). Our enemy is not other people, but rather evil itself and the sin in and around us.

12. We can expect our power (in ourselves) to be broken (12:7b). We can expect to be purified, made spotless, and refined (12:10). And ultimately, we can expect to receive our allotted inheritance in God's kingdom (12:13). Paul models the importance of praying for one another in Ephesians 1:15–21. It is through prayer that we have access to God through the Holy Spirit that he has given to us. That Spirit gives us wisdom, hope, and incomparably great power—the same power that "raised Christ from the dead and seated him at [God's] right hand in the heavenly realms" (Eph. 1:20), so that we can endure to the end.

The NIV Application Commentary

Daniel

Tremper Longman III

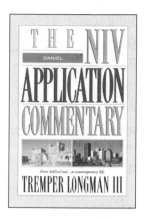

Most Bible commentaries take us on a one-way trip from our world to the world of the Bible. But they leave us there, assuming that we can some-how make the return journey on our own. In other words, they focus on the original meaning of the passage but don't discuss its contemporary application. The information they offer is valuable—but the job is only half done!

The NIV Application Commentary series helps us with both halves of the interpretive task. This new and unique series shows readers how to bring an ancient message into modern context. It explains not only what the Bible means but also how it can speak powerfully today.

"In spite of appearances, God is in control." That, Tremper Longman tells us over and over, is the core message of Daniel. What an appropriate message for Daniel's original hearers/readers, exiled in Babylon, and what an appropriate message for readers in the chaotic world of the twenty-first century as well.

Hardcover, Printed: 978-0-310-20608-8

Pick up a copy at your favorite bookstore or online!

Share Your Thoughts

With the Author: Your comments will be forwarded to
the author when you send them to *zauthor@zondervan.com*.

With Zondervan: Submit your review of this book
by writing to *zreview@zondervan.com*.

Free Online Resources at
www.zondervan.com

Zondervan AuthorTracker: Be notified whenever your favorite
authors publish new books, go on tour, or post an update
about what's happening in their lives at www.zondervan.com/
authortracker.

Daily Bible Verses and Devotions: Enrich your life with daily
Bible verses or devotions that help you start every morning
focused on God. Visit www.zondervan.com/newsletters.

Free Email Publications: Sign up for newsletters on Christian
living, academic resources, church ministry, fiction, children's
resources, and more. Visit www.zondervan.com/newsletters.

Zondervan Bible Search: Find and compare Bible passages in
a variety of translations at www.zondervanbiblesearch.com.

Other Benefits: Register yourself to receive online benefits
like coupons and special offers, or to participate in research.

ZONDERVAN®

ZONDERVAN.com/
AUTHORTRACKER
follow your favorite authors